THE ASHLEY DICTIONARY

ÉDITIONS RÉNYI INC.

355 Adelaide Street West, Suite 400, Toronto, Ontario Canada M5V 1S2

The Ashley Picture Dictionary

Illustrated by Kathryn Adams, Pat Gangnon, Colin Gillies, David Shaw and Yvonne Zan.
Cover illustration by Colin Gillies. Designed by David Shaw and Associates.

Typesetting by Osgoode Technical Translations

Color separations by New Concept Limited

Printed in Singapore by Khai Wah Litho Pte Limited

Edited by K. L. Cordner, P. O'Brien-Hitching, R. LeBel, P. Rényi.

The Ashley Picture Dictionary   ISBN 0-921606-46-X

INTRODUCTION

Some of Canada's best illustrators have contributed to this dictionary, which has been carefully designed to appeal to children, so that learning new words can be a pleasure.

Its unusually large number of terms – 3336 – makes the dictionary a flexible teaching tool. Because the vocabulary it encompasses is so broad, this dictionary can also be used to teach English as a Second Language to older children and adults, as well as helping young children acquire language skills.

NOTE TO TEACHERS AND PARENTS

In a children's dictionary, the most difficult decision is usually which words to include and which ones to leave out. Here, word selection has been based partly on word frequency analysis of English usage (in order to include the most commonly used terms), and partly on thematic clustering (in order to cover major fields of activity or interest).

This process was further complicated by the decision to systematically illustrate the meanings. Although the degree of abstraction has been kept reasonably low, it was deemed necessary to include terms such as "to expect" and "to forgive", which are virtually impossible to illustrate, given the space and other constraints. Instead of dropping these words, we decided to provide explanatory sentences that create a context.

Where variations occur between British and North-American English, both terms are given with an asterisk marking the British version (favor/favour*, gas/petrol*). Both variants are listed alphabetically in the index.

The alphabetical index at the end of the book lists every term in the dictionary with the number of its corresponding illustration. Teachers could use this feature to expand children's numeracy skills, by asking the child to match an index number with the actual illustration, as well as using it to train students in dictionary skills.

Great care has been taken to ensure that any contextual statements made are factual, have some educational value and are compatible with statements made elsewhere in the book. Lastly, from a strictly psychological viewpoint, the little girl featured in the book has not been made into a paragon of virtue; children will readily identify with her imperfections.

TO MY NEW FRIENDS

My name is Ashley. I am a little girl. I go to school, I am learning to swim, I have a little brother and many, many ideas. If you want to meet my father, the admiral, look at the page on the right. You will see him at the bottom of the page. My mother is on the next page, at the top. If you want to meet me, look up the word ''calm''.

Some people think dictionaries are dull. I guess they have not seen this one, which is all about me and the people I know.

Five grown-up illustrators had a lot of fun drawing the pictures. I also drew a picture (the zebra). Can you find it?

I must go now. Look for me in the dictionary.

Ashley

P.S. If you want to write to me about our dictionary, ask your parents or your teacher for my address.

1   abacus

Tell me **about** it.

It takes **about** an hour.

Jack went **about** his work.

2   about

The apple is **above** her head.

3   above

Paul is **absent** today.

4   absent

Every car has an **accelerator.**

5   accelerator

Jacques speaks with a French **accent.**

Put the **accent** on the first syllable.

6   accent

7   accident

8   accordion

They all **accused** Nancy.

9   to accuse

The **ace** of spades

10   ace

11   My head **aches.**

Acid can burn your skin.

12   acid

Oak trees grow from **acorns.**

13   acorn

14   acrobat

Paul lives **across** the road.

He came **across** an old friend yesterday.

15   across

Add them together.

16   to add

This is Ashley's **address.**

17   address

Ashley's father is an **admiral.**

18   admiral

I **adore** you.

19   to adore

Adults are grown-ups.

20   adult

Advance your king.

21   to **advance**

Is it an **advantage** to be tall?

22   advantage

Ashley's mum loves **adventure**.

23   adventure

He is **afraid**.

24   He is **afraid**.

Africa is a continent.

25   Africa

You can play **after** dinner.

Repeat **after** me!

Run **after** the ball!

26   after

Afternoon starts at 12 o'clock.

27   afternoon

Play it **again**, Sam!

Then **again**, you could play something different...

28   again

Tigger rubs **against** Jim's leg.

29   to rub **against**

What a difference in **age**!

30   age

Athletes are very **agile**.

31   **agile** person

32   aground

Reg is going **ahead** with his plans.

Plan **ahead** for your next holiday.

Helen is **ahead** of Jane in reading.

33   ahead

34   to provide **aid**

Is she **aiming** straight?

35   to **aim**

The kite is flying in the **air**.

36   air

37   air mattress

Insect in an **airtight** container

38   airtight

This **aeroplane** seems to be in trouble.

39   airplane/aeroplane*

Planes land at the **airport**.

40   airport

You can walk down the **aisle**.

41   aisle

42   alarm clock

A photo **album**

43   album

The house is **alight**!

44   alight

One fish is definitely **alive**.

45   alive

46   I want them **all**.

A cat in the back **alley**

47   alley

48   alligator

49   almond

Spot can **almost** reach the bone.

50   almost

Why is he sitting **alone**?

51   alone

Come **along** with me!

52   along

53   aloud

A B C D E F G H I J
K L M N O P Q R S
T U V W X Y Z

a b c d e f g h i j k l m
n o p q r s t u v w x y z

54   alphabet

55   Do I have to go **already**?

It hurts, but I am **alright**.

56   I am **alright**.

57   I **also** want some.

58   aluminum/aluminium* ladder

You should **always** be careful.

59   I **always** fall down.

60   ambulance

61   wolf **among** sheep

62   anchor

Ancient ruins

63   ancient

64   angle

Why is Spud **angry**?

65   He is **angry**.

66   animals

67   ankle

Mark **announces** the start of the race.

68   to **announce**

69   **another** sandwich

70   The **answer** is…

71   ant

72   Antarctic

73   antelope

74   antlers

75 I do not have **any** money.

76   It eats **anything**.

Spud is angry because…

77 He cannot go **anywhere**.

One is **apart** from the bunch.

78   apart

79   ape

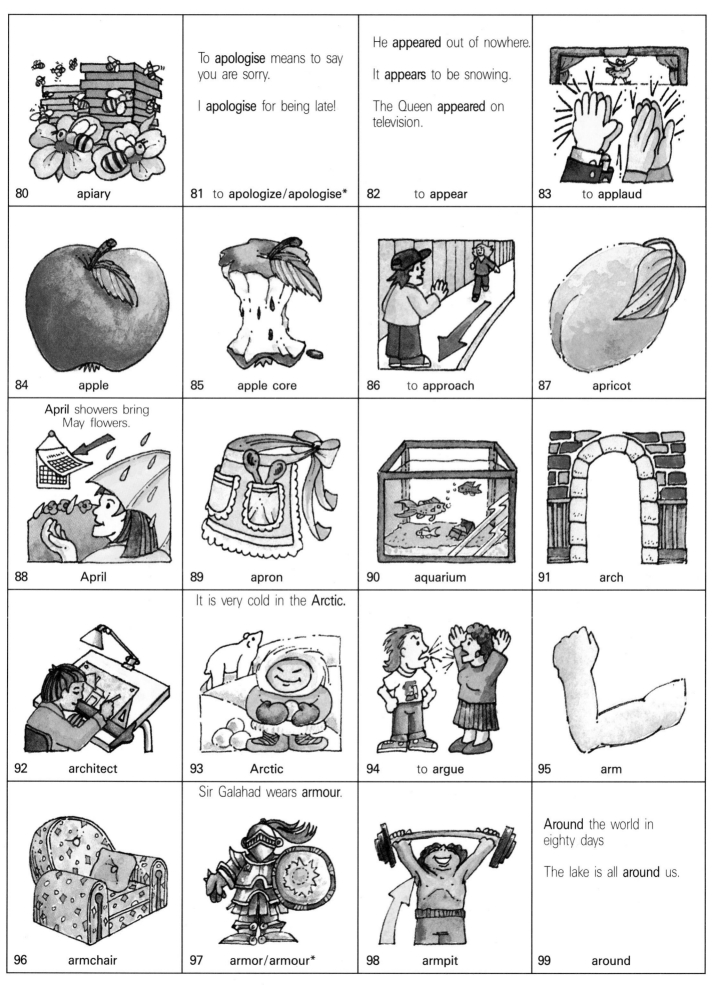

80 apiary	To **apologise** means to say you are sorry. I **apologise** for being late! 81 to **apologize/apologise***	He **appeared** out of nowhere. It **appears** to be snowing. The Queen **appeared** on television. 82 to **appear**	83 to **applaud**
84 apple	85 apple core	86 to **approach**	87 apricot
April showers bring May flowers. 88 April	89 apron	90 aquarium	91 arch
92 architect	It is very cold in the **Arctic.** 93 Arctic	94 to **argue**	95 arm
96 armchair	Sir Galahad wears **armour.** 97 armor/armour*	98 armpit	**Around** the world in eighty days The lake is all **around** us. 99 around

100 to **arrange** flowers	The police **arrested** Spud. 101 to **arrest**	102 to **arrive**	103 **arrow**
104 **artichoke**	Clare wants to become an **artist**. 105 **artist**	As soon as you like. As for you, I think you are in trouble! As pretty as a picture 106 **as**	107 **ash**
108 **ashtray**	**Asia** is a continent. 109 **Asia**	110 to **ask** for directions	Mary and Fluffy are both sound **asleep**. 111 **asleep**
112 **asparagus**	Two **aspirins** might help. 113 **aspirin**	Gary has **astonished** Jane. 114 to **astonish**	115 **astronaut**
116 **astronomer**	Helen is **at** home with her dad. They are looking **at** the picture. Go to bed **at** once! 117 **at**	118 **athlete**	Can you find your country in this **atlas?** 119 **atlas**

The **atmosphere** of the Earth

120   atmosphere

121   atom

122   to **attach**

123   Pay **attention**!

What do you store in the **attic**?

124   attic

125   audience

August is the eighth month of the year.

126   August

127   My **aunt** is my mother's sister.

Australia is an island continent.

128   Australia

129   author

An **automatic** awakening

130   automatic

Autumn is one of the four seasons.

131   autumn

132   avalanche

133   avocado

Why is Spud wide **awake**?

134   awake

135   She is **away**.

136   an **awful** smell

137   an **awkward** person

138   axe

The **axle** links two wheels.

139   axle

B

Babies are cute!

140   baby

141   baby carriage

Scratch my **back**!

142   back

144   **bacon** and eggs

145   **bad** apple

146   badge

143   to **back up**

What is inside the **bag**?

147   bag

The **bait** attracts the mouse.

148   bait

149   to bake

150   baker

151   bakery

152   good balance

153   balcony

Tom is **bald**.

154   bald

155   ball

156   ballerina

157   ballet

158   balloon

159 hot air **balloon**

160 **banana**

This **band** is a headband.

161 **band**

162 musical **band**

A **bandage** made it feel better.

163 **bandage**

164 to **bang**

Sliding down the **banister**

165 **banister**

Do you have a **bank** account?

166 **bank**

167 **bar**

Pubs are for adults!

168 **bar**

169 **barbed** wire

The **barber** cuts Michael's hair.

170 **barber**

171 one **bare** foot

A **bargain** at this price

172 **bargain**

Barges travel along the canals.

173 **barge**

174 to **bark**

Barley is grown on the farm.

176 **barley**

177 **barn**

Soldiers live in **barracks.**

178 **barracks**

175 **bark**

A **barrel** of olive oil

179   barrel

The **barrel** of a gun

180   barrel

181   barrette

182   barrier

The **base** of a column

183   base

A baseball **base**

184   base

185   baseball

186   basement

187   basil

188   basket

189   basketball

A baseball **bat**

190   bats

192   I am taking a **bath.**

193   bathroom

194   bathtub

Bats fly at night.

191   bat

A **battery** for your radio

195   battery

196   bay

Mother uses **bay leaves** for cooking.

197   bay leaves

198   bazaar

Do you promise to **be** good?

I **am** good.

Tom and Bob **are** good, but **is** Ashley good?

199   to **be**

200   beach

A whole string of **beads**

201   bead

202   beak

203   **beam** of light

204   beans

Billy the **bear** can ride a bicycle.

205   bear

A long **beard**

206   beard

What an awful-looking **beast**!

207   beast

Nellie **beats** the drum.

208   to **beat**

209   beautiful

Beavers build dams.

210   beaver

...I lost my cat.

211   I am crying **because**...

The caterpillar **becomes** a butterfly.

212   to **become**

213   bed

214   bed lamp

215   bedroom

The **bee** is a useful insect.

216   bee

217   beech

Bees live in **beehives**.

218   beehive

A mug of **beer**

219   beer

Beetroot grows in the ground.

220   beet

221   beetle

222 Wash your hands **before** dinner.

To **begin** with, let's have breakfast!

Ashley's piano lesson **begins** at ten o'clock.

Our piano lesson **begins** at nine o'clock.

223   to beg

224   to begin

Alice **behaves** well.

225   to behave

Julia hides **behind** the tree.

226   behind

227   beige

228 I **believe** in dragons.

229   bell

230   belly button

231 He **belongs** to me.

The cat is **below** the table.

232   below

233   belt

234   bench

A **bend** in the road

235   bend

236   to bend

237   beret

Pat stands **beside** the tree.

238   beside

Should you not eat something else **besides** dessert?

Besides, you should not eat so much sugar.

239   besides

240   best

Sheila writes **better** than Tom.

Tom is lazy, he can do **better.**

241   better

Phil walks **between** the rocks.

242   between

243   bib

244   bicycle

245   big

A **bike** is a bicycle.

246   bike

247   bill

248   billboard

Snooker is a game.

249   billiards

250   to bind

251   binoculars

252   bird

Ashley weighed seven pounds at **birth.**

The **birth** of a nation

The cat gave **birth** to four little kittens.

253   birth

Happy **birthday** to you!

254   birthday

255   biscuit

Fred **bites** into his sandwich.

256   to bite

He took a big **bite.**

257   bite

Beer has a **bitter** taste.

Ashley wept **bitter** tears when she lost her favourite doll.

258   bitter

| 259 black | 260 blackberry | There are many species of **blackbird**.
261 blackbird | Colin drew this on the **blackboard**.
262 blackboard |

263 blackcurrant

264 blacksmith

The **blade** is sharp!
265 blade

Father **blamed** Ashley, but she did not do it.

Father should **blame** Crispin, who did do it!

266 to blame

267 blank page

268 blanket

A **blast** is an explosion.
269 blast

270 to blast

The firefighters put out the **blaze**.
271 blaze

272 blazer

Bleach helps clean the laundry.
273 bleach

Her nose is **bleeding**.
274 to bleed

275 blender

The **blind** cannot see.
276 blind

277 to blink

Blisters hurt!
278 blister

279   blizzard

Do you play with **blocks**?

280   block

The car is going round the **block**.

281   a city **block**

The policeman **blocks** John's way.

282   to **block**

Blonde hair

283   **blond** hair

A **blood** transfusion

284   blood

The flower is in full **bloom**.

285   bloom

286   to **blossom**

An ink **blot**

287   blot

288   blouse

289   a **blow** to the head

290   to **blow**

291   blue

292   blueberries

This knife is too **blunt** to cut the tomato.

Sometimes it is better to be **blunt** when giving your friend the bad news.

293   blunt

Cora **blushes** easily.

294   to **blush**

295   boar

296   board

Christopher likes to **boast**.

His modesty is nothing to **boast** about.

297   to **boast**

298   boat

299 bobby pin	The human **body** 300 body	301 to **boil**	302 bolt
A **bone** for the dog 303 bone	304 bonfire	305 book	306 bookshelf
307 boomerang	308 boot	**Border** between two countries 309 border	It is hard to **bore** a hole in concrete. 310 to **bore**
What year were you **born**? She is a **born** leader. 312 born	Can I **borrow** some money? Ashley often **borrows** her brother's bike. 313 to **borrow**	314 boss	Ashley can **bore** people to death. Bob **bores** me because he talks too much. 311 to **bore**
Mel and Chip are **both** cute. **Both** today and tomorrow· 315 both	316 bottle	317 bottle opener	318 bottom

A **boulder** is a large piece of rock.

319   boulder

It **bounces** on the ground.

320   to bounce

A **bouquet** of flowers

321   bouquet

Bow and arrow

322   bow

324   bowl

What is inside the **box**?

325   box

326   boxer

323   bow tie

327   boy

328   bra

329   bracelet

Carla **brags** about her new toys.

Her dad tells her not to **brag.**

330   to brag

We use our **brains** to think.

331   brain

Every car has **brakes.**

332   brake

333   to brake

The **branch** of a big tree

334   branch

The dentist said you were very **brave.**

335   brave

336   bread

337   to break

338   to break down

A robber **broke in**.

339   to break in

We eat **breakfast** in the morning.

340   breakfast

Dragons have hot **breath**.

341   bad breath

342   to breathe

Is your house made of **bricks**?

343   brick

Pam is building a **brick** wall.

344   bricklayer

The **bride** is shy.

345   bride

So is the **bridegroom**.

346   bridegroom

347   bridge

A **bridle** for the horse

348   bridle

349   briefcase

350   bright sun

Torp **brings** my slippers.

351   to bring

Ashley **brings** back her library books.

352   to bring back

353   brittle glass

354   broccoli

355   brooch

A **brook** is a small river.

356   brook

357   broom

358   I love my **brother**.

359 brow	360 brown

Sean needs to **brush** his hair.

362   to **brush**   363   **brush**

That is a bad **bruise.**

361   bruise

366   brussels sprouts

364   paint**brush**

365   tooth**brush**

367   bubble

368   bucket

369   belt **buckle**

370   bud

371   buffalo

372   bug

The soldier plays the **bugle.**

373   bugle

374   to **build**

375   bull

376   bulldozer

Bullets are dangerous.

377   bullet

378   bullhorn

Charlie is a big **bully**.

379   bully

380   bump

381   bumpers

A **bunch** of asparagus

382   bunch

383   bundle

384   buoy

385   burglar

The fire **burns** brightly.

386   to burn

His balloon **burst**.

387   to burst

388   to bury

389   bus

390   bus stop

A **bush** is smaller than a tree.

391   bush

392   I am busy now.

I would like to go, **but** I am busy.

Paul is big, **but** his sister is bigger.

But for you, we would have lost the game.

393   but

394   butcher

Some **butter** for my bread

395   butter

396   butterfly

397   buttons

Phil **buys** an ice cream.

398   to buy

C

399   cabbage

A **cabin** in the forest

400   cabin

401   cabinet

402   cable

403   cactus

404   cage

405   cake

406   calculator

407   calendar

408   calf

409   to **call**

Ashley is always **calm**.

412   She is **calm**.

413   camel

414   camera

We will **call off** the picnic if it rains.

Ashley has **called off** our trip to the zoo.

410   to **call off**

They are **camping** together.

415   to **camp**

416   campsite

417   can

411   to **call up**

418   can opener

Ships travel through the **canal**.

419   canal

420   canary

421   candle

422   candlestick

423   candy

Grandpa uses a **walking stick**.

424   cane

425   cannon

426   I **cannot** see.

427   canoe

Cantaloupe is a type of melon.

428   cantaloupe

The river is in the **canyon**.

429   canyon

430   cap

A **cape** is the narrow tip of a continent.

431   cape

432   cape

M is a **capital** letter.

Paris is the **capital** of France.

The money you have saved up is your **capital**.

433   capital

He is the **captain** of his ship.

434   captain

435   to **capture**

436   car

A **caravan** crosses the desert.

437   caravan

438   cards

This box is made of **cardboard**.

439   cardboard

The nurse **cares** for the sick.

440   to **care**

Careless today, sorry tomorrow.

441   He is **careless**.

442   cargo

443   carnation

A **carnival** is one big party.

444   carnival

445   carpenter

446   carpet

447   carriage

448   carrot

Mr. Brown always **carries** too much.

449   to **carry**

450   cart

A **carton** of screws

451   carton

452   to carve

453   case

Cash is money.

454   cash

455   cashews

456   castle

457   cat

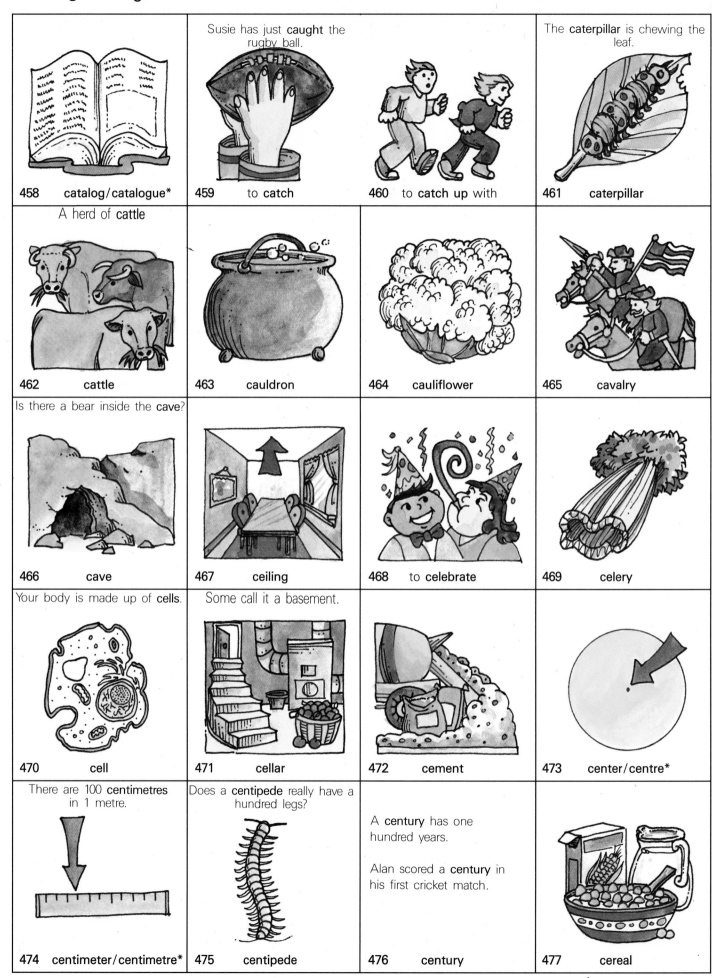

458 catalog/catalogue*

Susie has just **caught** the rugby ball.

459 to **catch**

460 to **catch up** with

The **caterpillar** is chewing the leaf.

461 caterpillar

A herd of **cattle**

462 cattle

463 cauldron

464 cauliflower

465 cavalry

Is there a bear inside the **cave**?

466 cave

467 ceiling

468 to **celebrate**

469 celery

Your body is made up of **cells**.

470 cell

Some call it a basement.

471 cellar

472 cement

473 center/centre*

There are 100 **centimetres** in 1 metre.

474 centimeter/centimetre*

Does a **centipede** really have a hundred legs?

475 centipede

A **century** has one hundred years.

Alan scored a **century** in his first cricket match.

476 century

477 cereal

Ashley is **certain** that she is right.

She has a **certain** feeling about Tim, but she can't quite explain why.

478   certain

479   certificate

480   chain

481   chainsaw

482   chair

483   chalk

484   champion

This is the **change** I got from a £5 note.

485   change

487   channel

This book has many **chapters**.

488   chapter

Ashley has a strong **character**.

She is quite a **character**.

What does this **character** mean?

489   character

Carl **changed** his clothes.

486   to change

490   charcoal

Chard is a kind of vegetable.

491   chard

The police **charged** Spud with robbery.

Your toy has stopped because I forgot to **charge** the battery.

They **charged** me a lot of money for this coat.

492   to charge

493   chariot

494   chart

495   to chase

496   to chat

497   **cheap** pencil, expensive crown

Gary is trying to **cheat** by looking at Mary's answers.

498   to **cheat**

Did you **check** your watch this morning?

499   to **check**

500   **cheek**

Cheese is made from milk.

501   **cheese**

Cheques are used to pay for things.

502   **cheque***/**check**

503   **cherries**

His waistcoat barely covers his **chest**.

504   **chest**

505   **chestnut**

Chew well before you swallow.

506   to **chew**

507   **chick peas**

508   **chicken**

509   **chicken-pox**

The **chief** is saluting.

510   **chief**

511   **child**

512   a **chilly** day

513   **chimney**

514   **chimpanzee**

515   **chin**

516   **china**

A **chip** never falls far from the tree.

517   **chip**

The sculptor uses a **chisel.**

518　　chisel

Chives taste like onions.

519　　chives

A **chocolate** bar

520　　chocolate

Do you sing in a **choir?**

521　　choir

Choking someone is not a joke.

522　　to **choke**

Peter **choked** on the bone.

523　　to **choke on**

Which one should I **choose?**

524　　to **choose**

Chopping onions

525　　to **chop**

526　　chopsticks

Chrome is a type of metal.

527　　chrome

528　　chrysanthemum

529　　a **chunk** of coal

This **cigar** stinks!

530　　cigar

Cigarettes make you sick.

531　　cigarette

532　　circle

533　　circus

Do you live in a big **city?**

534　　city

A **clam** lives in its shell.

535　　clam

Held together with a **clamp**

536　　clamp

537　　to **clap**

538   classroom

The crab has strong **claws**.

539   claw

Clay is used to make bricks.

You can also make pots and dishes out of **clay**.

540   clay

541 She is all **clean**.

Aunt Betty **clears** the table.

542   to clear

543   cliff

Climbing to the top

544   to climb

545   clinic

546   to clip

547   clock

548   to close

Do you keep your **cupboard** neat?

549   closet

Clothes are made out of **cloth**.

There is a table**cloth** on the table.

I need a fresh drying-up **cloth** for all these dishes.

550   cloth

551   clothes

552   clothesline

553   cloud

A four-leaf **clover** is lucky.

554   clover

555   clown

Thal uses his **club** to hunt.

556   club

The police found a **clue** to the crime.

Sheila does not have a **clue** how to get there.

I will give you a **clue**.

557   clue

The **clutch** pedal is on the left.

558   clutch

Clutch the rope tightly!

559   to **clutch**

Meet my **coach**.

560   coach

We are travelling by **coach**.

561   coach

Coal comes from a mine.

563   coal

This cloth is very **coarse**.

Do not use **coarse** language!

564   coarse

565   coast

Priscilla **coaches** the team twice a week.

562   to **coach**

You need a warm **coat** in winter.

566   coat

A **cobweb** is the spider's home.

567   cobweb

568   cocoa

569   coconut

570   cod

Coffee beans grow on trees.

571   coffee

572   coffin

573   coil

574   coin

575   I am **cold**.

576   collar

Ashley's sister **collects** stamps.

577   to **collect**

College is a school for bigger children and adults.

578   college

579 Cars **collide** when drivers sleep.

580   collision

A bad **collision**

Which is your favourite **colour?**

581   colors/colours*

A mare and her **colt**

582   colt

Stone **columns**

583   column

584   comb

585   to comb

Combine them together.

586   to combine

Tell Gordon to **come** home.

Ashley **came** to the party by bus.

Do you **come** here often?

Come on, tell me!

587   to come

It **came off** in my hand.

588   to come off

He fainted, but quickly **came to.**

589   to come to

590   comfortable

A real **comma** is smaller than this.

591   comma

592   to command

We live in a small **community**.

There is a pool at the **community** centre.

Building the centre was a **community** effort.

593   community

Tom is Tim's **companion.**

594   companions

595 I am in good **company.**

596   to compare

All **compasses** point North!

597 My **compass** points North.

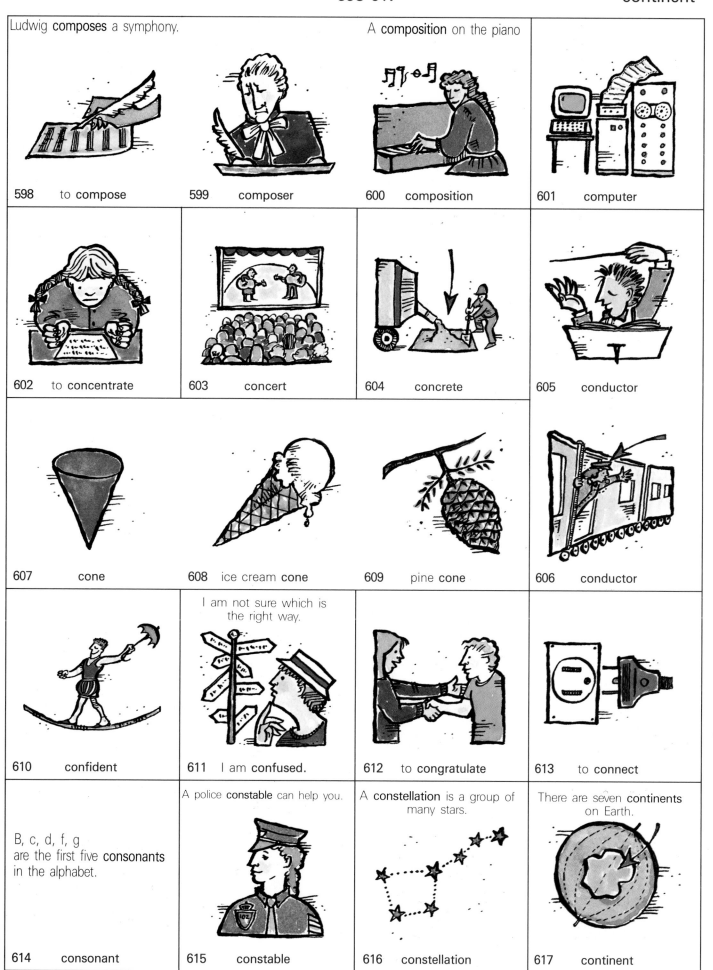

Ludwig **composes** a symphony.

A **composition** on the piano

598   to **compose**

599   **composer**

600   **composition**

601   **computer**

602   to **concentrate**

603   **concert**

604   **concrete**

605   **conductor**

607   **cone**

608   ice cream **cone**

609   pine **cone**

606   **conductor**

610   **confident**

I am not sure which is the right way.

611   I am **confused.**

612   to **congratulate**

613   to **connect**

B, c, d, f, g
are the first five **consonants**
in the alphabet.

A police **constable** can help you.

A **constellation** is a group of many stars.

There are seven **continents** on Earth.

614   **consonant**

615   **constable**

616   **constellation**

617   **continent**

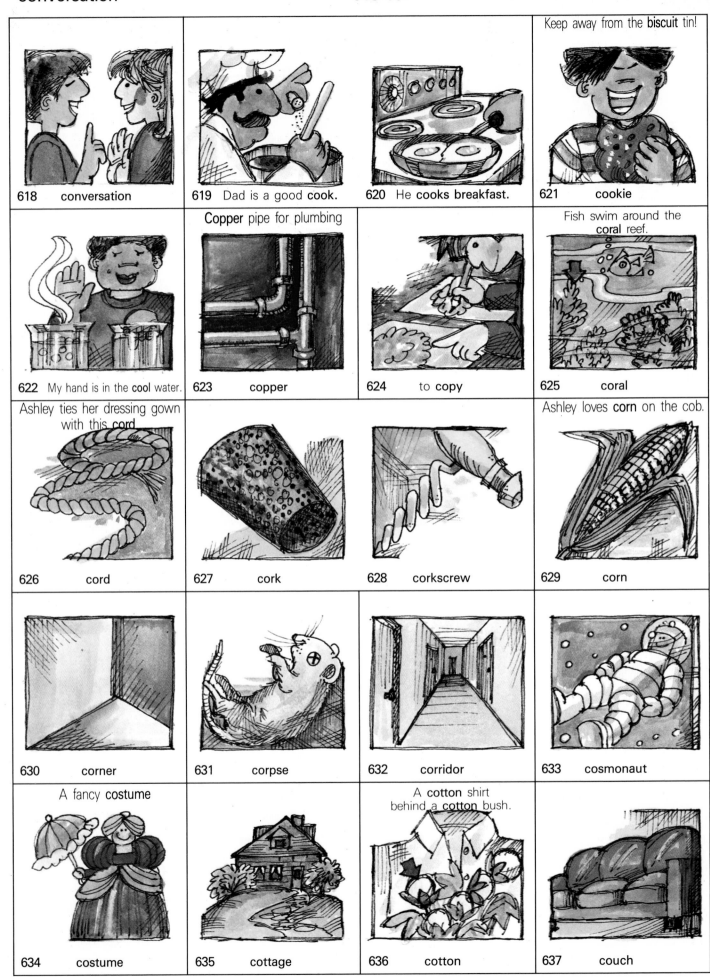

618   conversation

619   Dad is a good **cook**.

620   He **cooks** breakfast.

Keep away from the **biscuit** tin!

621   cookie

622   My hand is in the **cool** water.

Copper pipe for plumbing

623   copper

624   to **copy**

Fish swim around the **coral** reef.

625   coral

Ashley ties her dressing gown with this **cord**

626   cord

627   cork

628   corkscrew

Ashley loves **corn** on the cob.

629   corn

630   corner

631   corpse

632   corridor

633   cosmonaut

A fancy **costume**

634   costume

635   cottage

A **cotton** shirt behind a **cotton** bush.

636   cotton

637   couch

Kim **coughs** politely.

638　to cough

639　to count

640　counter

Put it on the **counter!**

641　counter

Have you been to the **country?**

642　country

This **country** is Canada.

643　country

Mum and Dad are a **couple.**

644　couple

It takes **courage** to fight dragons.

645　courage

A tennis **court**

646　court

647　My **cousin** is my uncle's daughter.

648　to cover

Keep the **cover** on the jar.

649　cover

650　cow

651　This boy is a **coward.**

652　cowboy

Crabs live in the sea.

653　crab

This jar has a **crack** in it.

654　crack

655　cracker

656　cradle

657　crane

658 crane	659 to crash

What is inside the **crate**?

660 crate

661 to crawl

662 crayfish

663 crayons

Dad likes **cream** in his coffee.

Ice **cream** is very sweet.

Sun **cream** protects your skin.

664 cream

665 crease

What a strange **creature**!

666 creature

A **creek** is a small river.

667 creek

668 the crew

669 crib

670 cricket

671 criminal

672 crocodile

Crocuses are a sign of spring.

673 crocus

That **crook** stole an apple!

674 crook

675 crooked post

The leaning picture of Pisa

676 crooked painting, upright tower

This farmer has grown a healthy **crop** of maize.

677 crop

Look before you **cross**!

678   cross

679   to **cross**

680   to **cross** out

681   crow

682   A big **crowd** in a small space.

683   crown

Sir Peter **crowns** the new Queen.

684   to **crown**

685   crumb

Crushing grapes for wine

686   to **crush**

Ashley likes the **crust** best.

687   crust

688   crutch

689   to **cry**

A **crystal** ball

690   crystal

A **cub** is a baby bear.

691   cub

692   cube

693   cuckoo

694   cucumber

695   cuff

A **cup** of tea

696   cup

The jar is in the **cupboard**.

697   cupboard

698 curb/kerb*

699 I am cured.

Samantha **curls** her hair.
700 to curl

Now she has **curly** hair.
701 curly

702 curious

703 currant

A strong **current**
704 current

705 curtains

706 curve

707 cushion

708 customer

709 to cut

712 cute

713 cutlery

714 cycle

710 to **cut in**

715 cylinder

716 cymbals

717 cypress

Cut out the paper doll !
711 to **cut out**

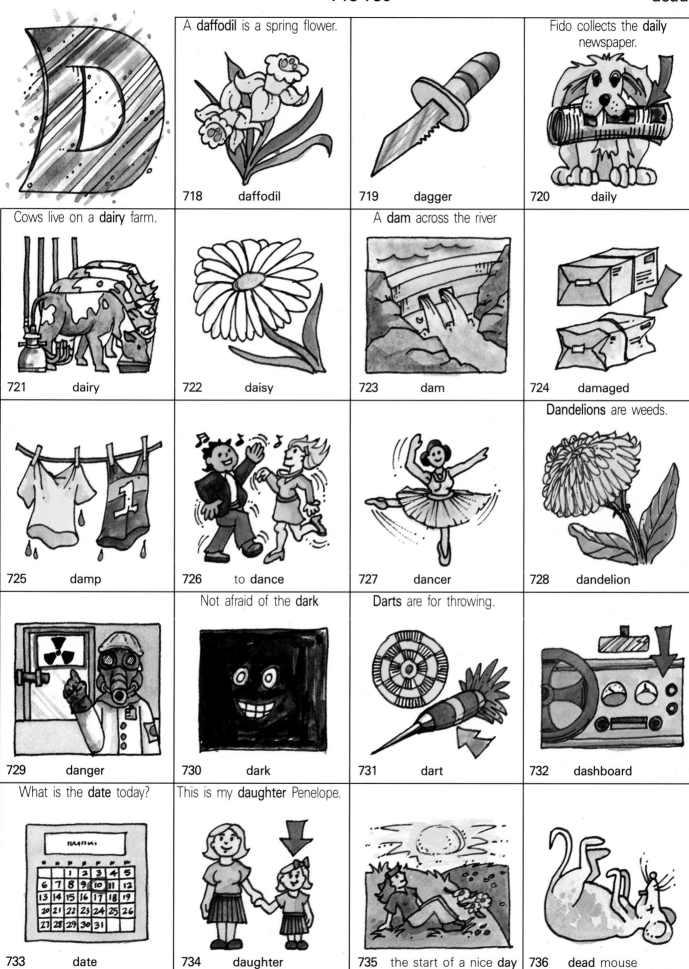

718   daffodil

A **daffodil** is a spring flower.

719   dagger

720   daily

Fido collects the **daily** newspaper.

Cows live on a **dairy** farm.

721   dairy

722   daisy

A **dam** across the river

723   dam

724   damaged

725   damp

726   to dance

727   dancer

Dandelions are weeds.

728   dandelion

729   danger

Not afraid of the **dark**

730   dark

Darts are for throwing.

731   dart

732   dashboard

What is the **date** today?

733   date

This is my **daughter** Penelope.

734   daughter

735   the start of a nice **day**

736   **dead** mouse

The **deaf** cannot hear.

737 deaf

Chuck is my **dear** friend.

Dear Mum, this trip is fun!

Oh **dear**, I forgot my purse.

738 dear

December is the last month of the year.

739 December

Ashley cannot **decide** what to wear.

Mum may have to **decide** for her.

740 to decide

The **deck** of a ship

741 deck

Phil the pirate **decorates** the tree.

742 to decorate

743 decoration

Albert avoids the **deep** end.

744 deep end

There are **deer** in the woods.

745 deer

746 to deliver

Tom **dented** my car.

747 to dent

748 dentist

749 department store

750 desert

Who put this **desk** in the desert?

751 desk

752 dessert

Godzilla **destroys** the city.

753 to destroy

A kind of warship

754 destroyer

755 detective

Morning **dew** on the leaves

756 dew

757 diagonal

758 diagram

Diamonds are precious stones which sparkle.
759 diamond

Babies need nappies.
760 diaper

Do you keep a diary?
761 diary

Look it up in the dictionary.
762 dictionary

763 to die

All people are born equal, there is no difference between them.

There is quite a difference between night and day.
764 difference

...but all equal
765 different people

766 to dig

Good luck, snake!
767 The snake digests an elephant.

A very dim room
768 dim

Ashley has dimples in her cheeks.
769 dimple

770 dinghy

771 dining room

772 dinner

773 dinosaur

This way!
774 direction

Daddy stepped into the dirt.
775 dirt

His trousers are really dirty.
776 dirty

I **disagree** with you, we have different opinions.

777   to **disagree**

The apple has **disappeared**.

778   to **disappear**

779   **disaster**

780   to **discover**

781   to **discuss**

782   **disease**

Ashley wears a **disguise**.

783   **disguise**

Please wash the **dishes**! Ashley, where are you?

784   **dishes**

785   a **dishonest** person

786   **dishwater**

787   to **dislike**

The tablet **dissolves** in water.

788   to **dissolve**

789   **distance** between two trees

A **distant** tree is far away.

790   a **distant** tree

The **district** where I live

791   **district**

We are digging a **ditch** to drain the field.

792   **ditch**

793   to **dive**

To **divide** an apple

794   to **divide**

795   I feel **dizzy**.

I have to **do** something to fix the stool.

796   What shall I **do**?

797 dock	798 doctor	799 dog	800 doll
801 dolphin	802 dome	The **donkey** carries a heavy load. 803 donkey	804 door
805 doorknob	806 double	807 dough	The **dove** is a symbol of peace. 808 dove
Ashley has a **down** pillow. 809 down	810 to doze	Twelve eggs to a **dozen** 811 dozen	Do not **drag** it in the dirt! 812 to drag
813 dragon	814 dragonfly	815 drain	Roy **draws** very well. 816 to draw

Raise the **drawbridge!**

817   drawbridge

Ashley's socks are not in this **drawer.**

818   drawer

Ron **dreams** even when he is not sleeping.

819   a nice **dream**

820   I **dream** of sheep.

821   dress

822   to **dress**

Maybe Ashley's socks are in this **chest of drawers.**

823   dresser

824   to **dribble**

It is no fun to **drift** on the ocean.

825   to **drift**

Pam **drills** tiny holes.

826   to **drill**

827   drill

828   drink

The tap is **dripping.**

830   to **drip**

831   I **drive** carefully.

832   crazy **driver**

829   to **drink**

The rain has become a light **drizzle.**

833   drizzle

834   to **drool**

One **drop** at a time

835   drop

Our guest **dropped** the glass.

836   to **drop**

Drop in to see me anytime.

837   to drop in

838   Dad drops off the cat at the vet.

He dropped out of the race.

839   to drop out

I am almost asleep.

840   I feel drowsy.

841   drum

842   dry

843   to dry

844   dry cleaner

Put the wet laundry in the dryer.

845   dryer

The duchess is married to the duke.

846   duchess

847   duck

A duel is not a good way to settle an argument.

848   duel

849   duke

A rubbish dump

850   dump

851   to dump

852   dumptruck

The thief has been locked in the dungeon a long time.

853   dungeon

854   dusk

855   dust

856   dwarf

Each rabbit has a carrot.

857 **Each** one has a carrot.

Eagles are rare and must be protected.

858 **eagle**

859 **ear**

Early morning sun

860 **early**

Mum **earns** a good wage.

Ashley has **earned** a holiday.

You must **earn** it before you spend it.

861 to **earn**

The planet **Earth**

862 **Earth**

Shovelling **earth**

863 **earth**

864 **earthquake**

865 **easel**

East and west are opposites.

866 **east**

867 Swimming is **easy.**

868 to **eat**

869 to **eat** breakfast

870 to **eat** lunch

871 to **eat** dinner

Hello..ello...lo...

872 **echo**

A solar **eclipse**

873 **eclipse**

874 The tree is at the **edge.**

875 **eel**

The hen laid an **egg.**

876   egg

877   eggplant

878   eight

879   eighth

Reg streches the **elastic.**

880   elastic

881   elbow

Elections are held to choose the government.

Who won the **election?**

The **election** was very close.

882   election

883   electrician

884   electricity

885   elephant

886   elevator

887   elk

888   elm

Stephen has **embarrassed** him.

889   to embarrass

890   to embrace

891   embroidery

892   emergency

893   The jar is **empty.**

The **end** of the road

894   This is the **end.**

Some day they will stop being **enemies.**

895   enemies

The **engine** of a car makes it go.

896   engine

897   engineer

898   to **enjoy**

899   **enormous** dinosaur

900   That is **enough**.

901   to **enter**

902   entrance

903   envelope

904   equal

The **equator** divides the Earth into two hemispheres.

905   equator

Ashley is running an **errand** for Dad.

906   errand

One **escalator** moves up and one moves down.

907   escalator

He barely **escaped**.

908   to **escape**

Europe is a continent.

909   Europe

910   evaporation

911   Four is an **even** number.

912   an **even** surface

913   evergreen

Ashley makes her bed almost **every** day.

Must Mum tell her **every** time?

914   every

Some **exams** are easy.

915   exam

916 to examine	Sometimes Ashley does not set a good **example**. Things are easier to understand when you give an **example**. 917 example	918 exclamation mark	919 Excuse me!

Karen **exercises** to stay healthy.

920   to exercise

To **exist** is to be.

Ashley said "There is no such thing", and she meant "It does not **exist**".

921   to exist

922   to exit

The balloon will **expand** until it bursts.

923   to expand

We **expect** you at two o'clock.

Dad **expects** you to be good.

Anne cannot **expect** any more.

924   to expect

An **expensive** watch costs a lot of money.

925   expensive

926   experiment

Marjorie is an **expert** on books.

927   expert

Let me **explain** it to you.

928   to explain

Charlie is **exploring** in the jungle.

929   to explore

930   explosion

A fire **extinguisher**

931   extinguisher

932   eye

933   eyebrow

934   eyeglasses

935   eyelash

Pam read a **fable** about the ant and the grasshopper.

936   **fable**

937   **face**

938   **factory**

Tom has **failed** his exams.

939   to **fail**

940   to **fail**

941   **fair**

The **fairy** will grant you a wish.

942   **fairy**

We have **faith** in you.

Ashley accepted it in good **faith**.

943   **faith**

This one is a **fake**, it is not genuine.

944   **fake** painting

The leaves fall in the **autumn**.

945   **fall**

946   to **fall**

They thought the house was on fire.

949   **false** alarm

These people are related to each other.

950   **family**

947   to **fall down**

948   to **fall off**

Marilyn is a **famous** star.

951   **famous** actress

952   **fan**

953   **fancy** clothes

954   **fang**

955   The city is **far** away.

956   Farewell !

Our food comes from the **farm**.
957   farm

958   farmer

959   fast

Never forget to **fasten** it!
960   I **fasten** my seatbelt.

Hector likes sugar.
961   fat

Drinking poison is **fatal**.
962   fatal

963   father

The **tap** is dripping.
964   faucet

They both say it is the other's **fault**.
965   Whose **fault** is it?

Can you do me a **favour**?

Ashley is kind and likes doing people **favours**.
966   favor/favour*

My **favourite** flavour
967   favorite/favourite*

968   to **fear** the worst

969   feast

A bird must have lost this **feather**.
970   feather

The second month of the year
971   February

Elaine **feeds** the baby.
972   to feed

973   I **feel** well.

The **female** bird lays the eggs.
974   female

975 fence

976 fender

977 fern

978 ferry

979 festival

Paul has a bad **fever**.

980 fever

981 **Few** people came.

982 field

Alice is **fifth**.

983 fifth

They are bad and **fight** a lot.

984 to fight

985 to file

986 to fill

A **film** for her camera

988 film

One **filthy** pig

989 filthy

That **fin** belongs to a shark.

990 fin

987 to **fill up**

A **fine** for speeding

991 fine

992 I am **fine**.

993 finger

994 fingerprint

Ashley's friend **finished** first.

995   to **finish**

Fir trees have needles.

996   fir

997   fire

998   fire engine

999   fire escape

Beware! Fireworks can be dangerous!

1000   firecracker

1001   fireman

1002   fireplace

Ashley has a **firm** handshake.

Penny's **firm** makes toys.

Dad's decision is **firm**, Tom cannot have another ice cream.

1003   firm

First in line

1004   first

1005   fish

1006   to **fish**

1007   fishhook

1008   fist

1009   five

Do you think he can **fix** it?

1010   to **fix**

A pirate **flag**

1011   flag

1012   flake

1013   flame

Tweeter is **flapping** his wings.

1014   to **flap**

A **flare** can light up the night.

1015   flare

1016   flash

1017   flashlight

1018   flask

1019   flat

To **flatten** dough

1020   to flatten

Which **flavour** do you like best?

1021   flavor/flavour*

Spot has a **flea** on his back.

1022   flea

Shelley **flees** for his life.

1023   to flee

1024   fleece

Quite a bit of **flesh**

1025   flesh

1026   to float

A **flock** of birds

1027   flock

1028   flood

1029   floor

Jack needs **flour** for baking.

1030   flour

The blood **flows** into his vein.

1031   to flow

1032   flower

Crispin is ill with the **flu**.

1033   flu

1034   fluff

Lemonade is a **fluid**.

1035   fluid

1036   fly

Do up your **fly**!

1037   fly

Birds and planes **fly**.

1038   to fly

1039   foam

You cannot see far in the **fog**.

1040   fog

Fold it this way.

1041   to fold

That goose **follows** Tom everywhere.

1042   to follow

1043   food

1044   foot

1045   football

Footprint in the snow

1046   footprint

I hear **footsteps** behind me.

1047   footsteps

One **for** all and all **for** one.

For better or **for** worse

But **for** you, we would have lost the game.

1048   for

1049   to force

1050   forehead

There are animals in the **forest**.

1051   forest

Our dog **forgets** his name.

Dad **forgot** to buy milk.

Forget it!

1052   to forget

I **forgive** you if you promise to be good.

Ashley **forgave** her dog for eating her favourite doll.

1053   to forgive

1054   fork

The soldiers are inside the **fort**.

Go **forward** until you reach the front door.

Ashley thinks he is too **forward**.

Are you looking **forward** to your birthday?

| 1055 forklift | 1056 form | 1057 fort | 1058 forward |

This **fossil** was once a fish.

The **foundation** of a house

| 1059 fossil | 1060 foul odor/odour* | 1061 foundation | 1062 fountain |

A sly **fox**

A **fraction** of the whole pie

Eggs are very **fragile**.

| 1063 fox | 1064 fraction | 1065 fragile | 1066 frame |

Do you have **freckles**, too?

Atuk's orange juice **froze**.

Picked **fresh** from the tree

| 1067 freckle | 1068 free | 1069 to freeze | 1070 fresh |

Friday is the last weekday.

Fridge means refrigerator.

Carla **frightens** him every time.

| 1071 Friday | 1072 fridge | 1073 friends | 1074 to frighten |

			There is **frost** on the window.
1075 frog	1076 I am **from** Mars.	1077 front	1078 frost
What is he **frowning** about?	**Fruit** is much better for you than chocolate.		
1079 to frown	1080 fruit	1081 to fry	1082 frying pan
			This **fund** helps the poor.
1083 Cars need **fuel**.	1084 full	1085 having fun	1086 charity fund
They went to the **funeral**.	Pour it through the **funnel**.	Mother does not think that is **funny**. A **funny** thing happened on the way to school. Ashley felt **funny** after eating that mushroom.	A **fur** coat in the summer
1087 funeral	1088 funnel	1089 funny	1090 fur coat
The house would be cold without a **boiler**.		A **fuse** is an electrical safety device.	Fluffy is a **furry** cat.
1091 furnace/boiler*	1092 furniture	1094 fuse	1093 furry

A **gale** is a strong wind.

1095   gale

The art **gallery**

1096   gallery

A horse can canter, **gallop** or trot.

1097   to gallop

Shelby enjoys **games**.

1098   game

A **gander** is a male goose.

1099   gander

A **gang** of villains

1100   gang

Ashley has a **gap** between her front teeth.

1101   gap

The car is in the **garage**.

1102   garage

1103   garbage

1104   garbage can

1105   vegetable **garden**

1106   to gargle

Garlic has a strong taste.

1107   garlic

A **garter** keeps stockings up.

1108   garter

The balloon was filled with **gas**.

Some **gases** are lighter than air.

Firefighters wear **gas** masks to protect themselves.

1109   gas

1110   gas

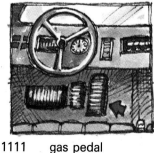

1111   gas pedal

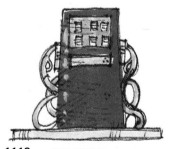

1112   gas pump

1113   gas station

1114　　gate

She is **gathering** flowers.

1115　　to **gather**

1116　　**gears**

1117　　**gem**

A high-ranking officer

1118　　**general**

1119　　a **generous** friend

1120　　a **gentle** person

Dad is a real **gentleman.**

1121　　**gentleman**

1122　　a **genuine** pig

We all study **geography.**

1123　　**geography**

Geraniums are common pot plants.

1124　　**geranium**

A pet **gerbil**

1125　　**gerbil**

Germs cause disease.

1126　　**germ**

Tigger the cat **gets** moving.

1127　　**Get** that mouse!

1128　I want to **get** it **back.**

Ashley **gets in** slowly.

1129　to **get in** the pool

Ashley **gets off...**

1130　　to **get off**

then on...

1131　　to **get on**

She **gets rid** of the rubbish...

1132　　to **get rid of**

...but first she **gets up.**

1133　　to **get up**

Are you afraid of **ghosts**?

1134 ghost

1135 giant

1136 gift

A **gigantic** whale

1137 gigantic

1138 to giggle

Fish breathe through **gills**.

1139 gills

Ginger is a spice.

1140 ginger

A tasty **gingerbread** man

1141 gingerbread

A **gipsy** caravan is always on the move.

1142 gipsy

Is a **giraffe** really higher than the sun?

1143 giraffe

1144 girl

She **gave** Anne the umbrella.

1145 to give

Glaciers are made of ice.

1148 glacier

1149 I am **glad**.

Windows are made of **glass**.

1150 glass

Anne **gave** it **back** when the rain stopped.

1146 to give back

Do you wear **glasses**?

1152 glasses

1153 to glide

A **glass** of water

1151 glass

1147 I **give up**!

A **glider** is a plane without an engine.

1154　　glider

1155　　gloves

Glue makes it stick.

1156　　glue

1157　　to **go**

The goalkeeper defends the **goal**.

1161　　goal

A billy**goat** or a nanny**goat**?

1162　　goat

The **goggles** protect her eyes.

1163　　goggles

He **goes down** to work.

1158　　to **go down**

A bar of **gold**

1164　　gold

1165　　goldfish

Uncle John plays **golf**.

1166　　golf

Spot **goes in** for a nap.

1159　　to **go in**

This food tastes **good**.

1167　　good

1168　　**Goodbye** Mom!

1169　　goose

Jack **goes up** the beanstalk.

1160　　to **go up**

1170　　gooseberry

She thinks she has a **gorgeous** hairdo.

1171　　gorgeous

1172　　gorilla

The government **governs** the country.

It is not as easy to **govern** a country as it seems.

There are rules **governing** how we play this game.

1173　　to **govern**

The **government** is elected by the people.

Ashley's dad, the admiral, works for the **government**.

1174 government

He **grabbed** her ice cream and will be punished.

1175 to grab

1176 He is very **gracious**.

This is my school and I am in second **form**.

1177 I am in **grade** one.

We harvest **grain** to make flour.

1178 grain

1000 **grams** = 1 kilogram

1179 gram

1180 grandchild

1181 grandfather

Ashley's **grandmother** likes baking.

1182 grandmother

Granite is a hard rock.

1183 granite

I **grant** you ten days' leave of absence.

The good fairy will **grant** you three wishes.

1184 to grant

A bunch of **grapes**

1185 grapes

1186 grapefruit

1187 graph

1188 grass

1189 grasshopper

1190 grater

1191 grave

Loose **gravel** next to the road

1192 gravel

1193 **Gravity** makes apples fall.

Cows **graze** in the field.

1194   to **graze**

Grease will stop the squeaking.

1195   **grease**

1196   a **great** toy

1197   **greedy**

1198   **green**

1199   **green** bean

1200   **greenhouse**

Tom always **greets** a lady.

1201   to **greet**

1202   **grey***/**gray**

1203   to **grill**

1204   **grimy**

Chuck **grins** because he is happy.

1205   to **grin**

Mum **minces** meat for dinner.

1206   to **grind**

Grip the handlebars tightly.

1207   to **grip**

1208   to **groan**

The **grocer** tells her where to look.

1209   **grocer**

The bride and **groom**

1211   **groom**

The **groom** takes care of the horse.

1212   **groom**

Pam is **grooming** herself.

1213   to **groom**

1210   shopping for **groceries**

This **gross** thing is overfed.

1214   groove

1215   gross

1216   ground

1217   groundhog

A **group** of people

1218   group

1219   to grow

1220   to growl

1221   grown-up

He **guides** the guest to his room.

His **guest** arrives to stay for the night.

Now, let me **guess**...

1222   to guard

1223   to guess

1224   guest

1225   to guide

Ashley says she did not do it - she is not **guilty**.

Who is **guilty** of this theft?

The thief who took the biscuit tin is certainly **guilty**.

Guinea pigs eat a lot.

A **gulf** is part of the sea almost enclosed by land.

1226   guilty

1227   guinea pig

1228   guitar

1229   Gulf of Mexico

Sea **gulls** live by the water.

Brush your **gums** to keep them healthy.

There are better habits than chewing **gum**.

The water flows in the **gutter**.

1230   gull

1231   gum

1232   gum

1233   gutter

1234   bad **habit**

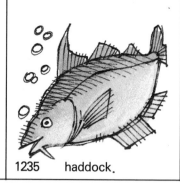

1235   **haddock**.

A sudden **hail** storm

1236   **hail**

Ashley's sister has lots of **hair**.

1237   **hair**

1238   **hairbrush**

1239   **hairdresser**

This is not a small **hairdryer**.

1240   **hairdryer**

Do you want the other **half**?

1241   **half**

This space is a **hall**.

1242   **hall**

Halloween is trick or treat night.

1243   **Halloween/Hallowe'en***

This space is a **corridor**.

1244   **hallway**

The soldier **halted** outside the door.

1245   to **halt**

Rob **hammered** in the nail.

1246   **hammer**

1247   to **hammer**

1248   **hammock**

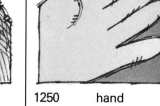

1249   **hamster**

1250   **hand**

1251   to **hand out**

Bicycles have **hand brakes**.

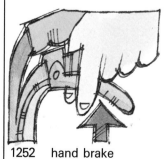

1252   **hand brake**

1253   handcuffs

Being blind is a **handicap**.

People can overcome any **handicap**.

1254   handicap

1255   handle

1256   handrail

He thinks he is very **handsome**.

1257   handsome

1258   handy person

Hang the picture straight!

1259   to hang

1260   to hang on

Aeroplanes are kept in a **hangar**.

1262   hangar

Hang your coat on the **hanger**.

1263   hanger

1264   handkerchief

1261   to hang up

1265   Accidents happen.

1266   He is happy.

The ship docked in the **harbour**.

1267   harbor/harbour*

Too **hard** to break

1268   hard

1269   hare

Never **harm** an animal !

1270   to harm

1271   harmonica

The horse is in a **harness**.

1272   harness

1273　harp

1274　a **harsh** winter

Sam **harvests** the crop.
1275　to **harvest**

1276　hat

The chick has **hatched**.
1277　to **hatch**

1278　hatchet

Michael **hauls** a heavy load.
1279　to **haul**

1280　**haunted** house

Pat **has** the doll Sharon wants.
1281　to **have**

1282　hawk

Hay for the horses
1283　hay

1284　**Haze** makes for a hazy day.

1285　hazel

1286　hazelnut

1287　head

1288　I have a **headache**.

1289　headrest

His broken leg is **healing**.
1290　to **heal**

1291　**healthy** flower

A big **pile** of rubbish
1292　heap

1293 I **hear** a voice.	1294 **heart**	1295 to **heat**	1296 **heater**
1297 to **heave**	1298 **heaven**	1299 one **heavy** elephant	A neat **hedge** round the garden is very nice. 1300 **hedge**
A **hedgehog** is not a porcupine. 1301 **hedgehog**	1302 **heel**	1303 **helicopter**	1304 **hell**
1305 **hello**	At the **helm** of the ship 1306 **helm**	Soldiers wear **helmets**. 1307 **helmet**	Gail's mum **helps** to start the car. 1308 to **help**
A small baby is **helpless**. 1309 **helpless**	1310 **hem**	The equator divides the Earth into two **hemispheres**. 1311 **hemisphere**	1312 **hen**

A **heptagon** has seven sides.

1313   heptagon

1314   herbs

A **herd** of cattle

1315   herd

1316   Come **here**!

A **hermit** lives alone.

1317   hermit

1318   hero

1319   heroine

1320   herring

Paul **hesitates** before diving in.

1321   to hesitate

A **hexagon** has six sides.

1322   hexagon

Bears **hibernate** all winter.

1323   to hibernate

1324   to hiccup

The **hide** of an animal is its skin.

1325   hide

1326   to hide

1327   hiding-place

1328   a **high** mountain

1329   high-rise

1330   high school

1331   highway

1332   to **hijack** a plane

There is a tree at the top of the **hill**.

1333   hill

1334   hinge

1335   hind legs

1336   hand on hip

Some call it a **hippo**.

1337   hippopotamus

1338   I study history.

Hit it straight on the head.

1339   to hit

Bees live in a bee**hive**.

1340   hive

1341   to hoard

1342   hoarse voice

Mum's **hobby** is knitting.

1343   hobby

My brother plays ice **hockey**.

1344   hockey

1347   hoe

Ashley is **holding** Tigger the cat.

1348   to hold

Ashley should not **hold** him **down** like that.

1349   to hold down

1345   hockey puck

1350   hole

Uncle Jack has worked hard for this **holiday**.

1351   holiday

Squirrels live in **hollow** trees.

1352   hollow tree

1346   hockey stick

Holly and its berries
1353   holly

In certain places cows are holy.
1354   a holy cow

The squirrels are at home.
1355 The squirrels are home.

1356   homework

Fred says he loves me.
1357   Is he honest?

Bears love honey.
1358   honey

1359   honeycomb

1360   honeydew melon

1361   to honk

1362   honor/honour*

Ashley's coat has a hood.
1363   hood

The engine is under the bonnet.
1364   hood

Horses have hooves.
1365   hoof

1366   hook

1367 jump through a hoop

1368   to hop

George hopes to be first.
1369   I hope to win.

One hopeless rider
1370   hopeless

1371   hopscotch

The sun rises over the horizon
1372   horizon

1373   horizontal

1374   horn

1375   French horn

1376   horn

A hornet can sting.

1377   hornet

1378   horse

Horseradish tastes hot!

1379   horseradish

A lucky horseshoe

1380   horseshoe

1381   hose

1382   hospital

It is really hot.

1383   hot

So hot, my tongue is burning.

1384   hot

We stay in hotels when we travel.

1386   hotel

One hour has sixty minutes.

1387   hour

1388   hourglass

How hot do you think it is?

1385   hot pepper

1389   house

A hovercraft travels over water and land.

1390   hovercraft

1391   I will show you how.

The wolf howls at the moon.

1392   to howl

1393   hub cap

1394   huckleberry

1395   to huddle

1396   huge

1397   hull

1398   hummingbird

1399   hump

1400   hundred

1401   She is **hungry**.

1402   to **hunt**

1403   to **hurl**

Who names the **hurricanes**?

1404   hurricane

1405   to **hurry**

1406   My wrist **hurts**.

Husband and wife

1407   husband

1408   hut

1409   hutch

1410   hyacinth

The choir sings a **hymn**.

1411   hymn

Hyphens are short lines between words that belong together.

1412   hyphen

Ice cubes in a glass

1413   ice

1414   ice cream

Icebergs can sink ships.

1415   iceberg

1416   icicle

Icing on the cake

1417   icing

I think she just had an **idea!**

1418   idea

Can you tell us apart?

1419   identical twins

1420   idiot

1421   idle

If I had a hammer, I would only hammer when no one was sleeping.

I would buy it for you **if** I could.

1422   if

1423   igloo

1424   ignition key

Paul has been **ill** for days.

1425   ill

1426   to illuminate

Pictures in a book are called **illustrations**.

This dictionary has many **illustrations**.

1427   illustration

This is an **important** matter.

What is **important** to Ashley may not be **important** to Jack.

1428   important

Is Tony **in?**

Go and jump **in** the lake!

In time, we will find out who took the biscuit tin.

1429   in

An **incense** burner

1430   incense

Twelve **inches** make a foot.

1431   inch

There is an **index** at the back of the book.

The **index** contains all the words in this dictionary.

1432   index

1433   indigo

Carla has decided to stay **indoors**.

1434   indoors

1435   infant

Aunt Sylvia has an **infection**.

1436   infection

Her condition is **infectious**.

You could catch an **infectious** disease.

Dad has an **infectious** laugh.

1437   . infectious

It is not nice to **inform** on someone.

1438   to inform

1439   The bear **inhabits** a cave.

What are your **initials**?

1440   initials

An **injection** in the arm

1441   injection

1442   injury

Ink is used for writing.

1443   ink

There are many different **insects**.

1444   insect

Inside the box

1445   inside

I **insist** that you have a bath.

1446   to insist

Fred **inspects** the leaf for disease.

1447   to inspect

A spoon for the soup

1449   Use a spoon **instead** of a fork!

Follow **instructions** to do the job properly.

1450   instruction

1451   instructor

1448   inspector

There is **insulation** in the walls of the house.

There is **insulation** around the wires so people will not get a shock.

1452   insulation

1453   intersection

She asked him why he wanted the job.

1454   interview

Daniel goes **into** the room.

1455   into the room

Marg **introduces** them to each other.

1456   to introduce

Vikings **invaded** other countries.

1457   to invade

Some became **invalids**.

1458   invalid

Did he really **invent** trees?

1459   to invent

The **invisible** man

1460   invisible

You are **invited** to our party.

1461   invitation

Please come!

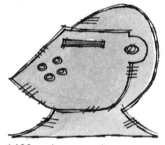

1462   He is inviting her.

1463   iris

Mel **irons** all his clothes.

1464   to iron

1465   iron

1466   iron mask

You can reach the **island** by boat.

1467   island

Ashley got a bad **itch** from the stinging nettles.

The **itch** will go away if she does not scratch.

1468   itch

1469   to itch

1470   My skin is itchy.

Ivy grows on walls.

1471   ivy

J

Luke **jabbed** me in the side.
1472   to **jab**

Is this **jacket** the right size?
1473   **jacket**

Some books have dust **jackets**.
1474   dust **jacket**

Be careful not to cut yourself!
1475   **jagged** edge

1476   **jail**/**gaol***

1477   **jam**

Martin **jammed** his foot in the door.
1478   to **jam**

The first month of the year
1479   **January**

1480   **jar**

This shark has **JAWS**.
1481   **jaw**

1482   **jeans**

1483   **jeep**

Jelly for dessert
1484   **jelly**

1485   **jet** engine

1486   **jet**

A precious **jewel**
1488   **jewel**

1489   **jigsaw puzzle**

1490   doing a **job**

1487   **jet** of water

The jockey rides a racehorse.

1491   jockey

1492   to jog

Join the ends together.

1493   to join

The elbow joint

1494   joint

Uncle Burt thinks this is a good joke.

1495   joke

The judge will decide.

1496   judge

1497   juggler

Fresh orange juice

1498   juice

July is the seventh month of the year.

1499   July

1500   to jump

1501   to jump in

1502   to jump on

Mel is a good jumper.

1503   jumper

1504   jumper

These are useful to start a car.

1505   jumper cables

June is a good time for tennis.

1506   June

There are tigers in the jungle.

1507   jungle

A junk is a Chinese boat.

1508   junk

Junk also means rubbish.

1509   junk

Ashley just got home.

Just a little, thanks.

The judge is a just person.

1510   just

1511   kaleidoscope

A kaleidoscope produces many beautiful patterns.

1512   kangaroo

1513   keel

The keel of a boat keeps it steady.

1514   kennel

Spot likes his kennel.

1515   kernel

1516   kettle

1517   key

1518   to kick

1519   kid

This kid is my friend.

1520   kid

Goats have kids too.

1521   to kidnap

Only criminals kidnap people.

1522   kidney

1523   to kill

A hunter killed the lion.

1524   kiln

Clay pots bake in a kiln.

1525   kilogram

1 kilogram = 1000 grams

1526   kilometer/kilometre*

1 kilometre = 1000 metres

1527   kilt

Men wear kilts in Scotland.

1528   A dress is a kind of garment.

1529   kind girl

		A newspaper **kiosk**	**Kippers** are a type of smoked herring.
1530 king	1531 kingfisher	1532 kiosk	1533 kippers

Give me a **kiss.**			Flying a **kite**
1534 to kiss	1535 kiss	1536 kitchen	1537 kite

The **kitten** will grow into a cat.			
1538 kitten	1539 kiwi	1540 knee	1541 to kneel

	Can you **knit** a sweater?	A door **knob**	**Knock** on the door.
1542 knife	1543 to knit	1544 knob	1545 to knock

	Do you **know** what it means? Ashley **knows** some French.		**Koalas** live in Australia.
1546 knot	1547 to know	1548 knuckle	1549 koala bear

There is a warning on the **label**.

1550   label

1551   laboratory

A fine **lace** collar

1552   lace

1554   ladder

1555   ladle

1556   lady

Bob **laces** up his shoes.

1553   to lace

1557   ladybug

Ladyfingers are cakes in America and vegetables in Britain.

1558   ladyfingers

The monster is in his **lair**.

1559   lair

Lakes are surrounded by land.

1560   lake

A **lamb** is a baby sheep.

1561   lamb

Flossie has a **lame** leg.

1562   lame

1563   lamp

1564   lamp-post

1565   lance

1566   land

1567   to land

1568   landing

The flat we live in belongs to our **landlord**.

We pay our **landlord** rent every month.

1569   landlord

Some motorways have many **lanes**.

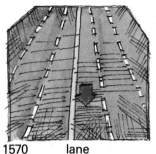

1570   lane

How many **languages** can you speak?

English is Ashley's first **language**.

Ashley wants to learn another **language**.

1571   language

1572   lantern

The baby is sitting on her **lap**.

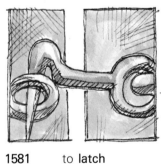

1573   lap

1574   larch

Lard is used for cooking.

1575   lard

1576   large

1577   lark

An eye**lash**

1578   lash

1579   the **last** piece

1580   Some things do **last**.

Latch the door, please.

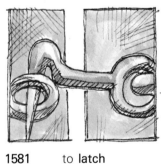

1581   to latch

People are upset when you are **late**.

1582   You are **late**.

Lather for shaving

1583   lather

1584   to laugh

The **launch** took Mr. and Mrs. Walker ashore.

1585   launch

1586   to launch

1587   launchpad

1588   dirty **laundry**

1589　　laundry

1590　　lavender

The **law** is the same for everybody.
1591　　Obey the **law**!

Did you mow the **lawn**?
1592　　lawn

1594　　to **lay** tiles

1595　**layer** upon **layer**

1596　　He is **lazy**.

1593　　lawn mower

Vincent **leads** the horse.
1597　　to **lead**

The **leader** of the group
1598　　leader

1599　　leaf

This bucket **leaks**.
1600　　to **leak**

The **leaning** tower of Pisa
1601　　to **lean**

1602　　I **learn** to read.

1603　　leash

1604　Shoes are made of **leather**.

I will just **leave** it here.
1605　　to **leave**

Tony is **leaving**.
1606　　to **leave**

1607　　ledge of a window

1608　　leek

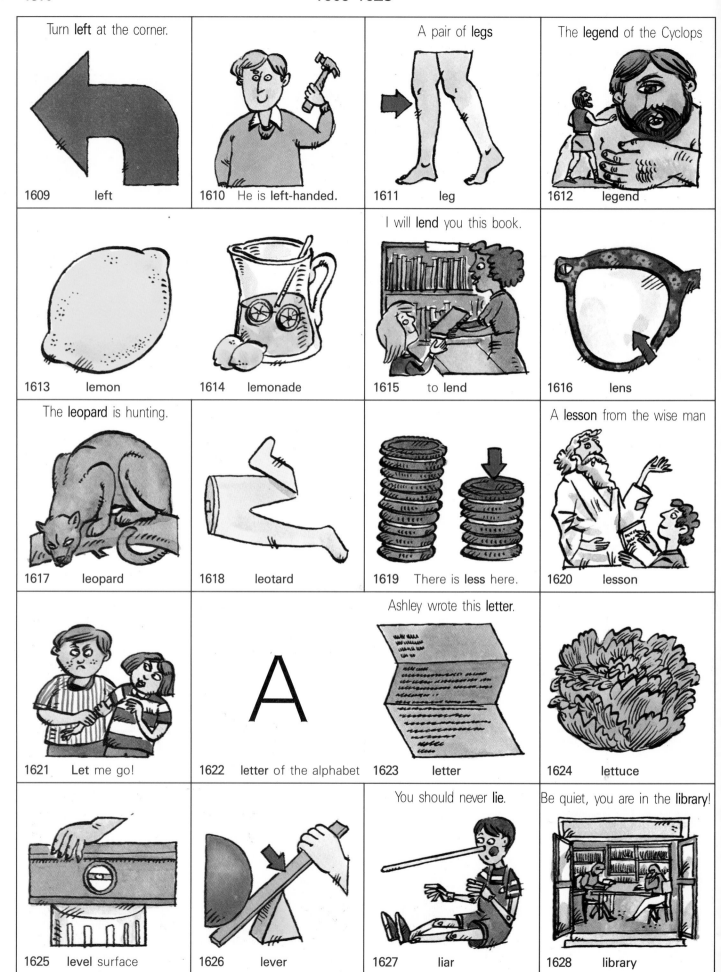

Turn **left** at the corner.

1609   left

1610   He is **left-handed**.

A pair of **legs**

1611   leg

The **legend** of the Cyclops

1612   legend

1613   lemon

1614   lemonade

I will **lend** you this book.

1615   to lend

1616   lens

The **leopard** is hunting.

1617   leopard

1618   leotard

There is **less** here.

1619   There is **less** here.

A **lesson** from the wise man

1620   lesson

1621   **Let** me go!

1622   letter of the alphabet

Ashley wrote this **letter**.

1623   letter

1624   lettuce

1625   **level** surface

1626   lever

You should never **lie**.

1627   liar

Be quiet, you are in the **library**!

1628   library

1629   licence plate

1630   to lick

The **lid** of the jar

1631   lid

I can tell if he is **lying**.

1632   to lie

This baby has just started his **life**.

1634   life

1635   lifeboat

1636   to lift

1633   to lie down

Dad **lights** the candle.

1637   light

1638   to light

1639   lightbulb

1640   She **lightens** the load.

1641   lighthouse

1642   lightning

1643   lightning rod

Sharon **likes** her cat.

1644   to like

Sophie is not **likely** to come tomorrow.

Ashley, that is a **likely** story!

1645   likely

Lilacs blossom in the spring.

1646   lilac

Easter **lilies**

1647   lily

The **limb** of a tree

1648   limb

1649 lime

There is a **limit** of three sweets for each child.

The speed **limit** is 30 miles per hour.

There is no **limit** to Joe's kindness.

1650 limit

Our neighbour walks with a **limp**.

1651 to limp

Can you draw a really straight **line**?

1652 line

1653 linen

An ocean **liner**

1654 liner

My jacket has a warm **lining**.

1655 lining

1656 to link

1657 lint

1658 lion

1659 lips

1660 lipstick

Water and milk are **liquids**.

1661 liquid

A **list** of things to do

1662 list

1663 They are **listening**.

A **litre** is a measure of volume.

1664 liter/litre*

Do not **litter**, ever!

1665 to litter

1666 a **little** apple

Ashley **lives** in the city.

Aunt Sally **lived** until she was seventy.

It would be difficult to **live** on the moon.

1667 to live

1668 lively

1669   living room

1670   lizard

Tim is **loading** the cannon.

1671   to **load**

They are **loading** the truck.

1672   to **load**

A fresh **loaf** of bread

1673   **loaf**

Colin **lent** Ashley some money because she had spent her allowance.

1674   to **loan**

1675   **lobster**

Did you **lock** the door?

1676   to **lock**

1678   **locomotive**

1679   **locust**

A ski **chalet** in the mountains

1680   **lodge**

There is a **lock** on the door.

1677   **lock**

1681   **loft**

1682   **log**

1683   **lollipop**

Eric is **lonely** because his friend has moved.

1684   **lonely**

The giraffe has a **long** neck.

1685   **long**

Frank **looks** longingly at the cakes.

1686   to **look**

Ashley weaves a scarf on her **loom.**

1687   **loom**

A **loop** in the rope

1688   **loop**

The strap is too **loose**.

1689   loose

Tony has **lost** a mitten.

1690   to **lose**

This **lotion** protects her skin.

1691   lotion

The **loud** music hurts Julia's ears.

1692   loud

1693   loudspeaker

1694   to **lounge**

Love is a very strong feeling.

Ashley says that if you have **love** you have everything.

1695   love

We **love** each other.

1696   to **love**

1697   lovely

1698   low branch

1699   to **lower**

Carl was very **lucky** to go on an adventure holiday.

Ashley is **lucky** to have such a cute little brother.

1700   lucky

Will all our clothes fit into the **luggage**?

1701   luggage

Lukewarm water is not hot and not cold.

1702   lukewarm water

Mum sings a **lullaby** to make the baby sleep.

1703   lullaby

1704   lumber

1705   lump

Susie is eating a sandwich for **lunch**.

1706   lunch

1707   lunchbox

Healthy **lungs** are important.

1708   lung

1709   magazine

1710   maggot

An unusual **magic** act.

1711   magic

1713   magnet

What a **magnificent** robe!

1714   magnificent

1715   magnifying glass

1712   magician

1716   magpie

1717   to mail

1718   mail carrier

What is Gus **making**?

1719   to make

Melody wears **makeup**.

1720   makeup

Male and female

1721   male

1722   mallet

Man and woman

1723   man

A **mandarin** orange

1724   mandarin

Ashley's uncle plays the **mandolin**.

1725   mandolin

The **mane** is the hair on the horse's neck.

1726   mane

The **mango** is a very sweet fruit.

1727   mango

1728 He has good **manners.**

1729 many

1730 map

Making a **marble** statue

1731 marble

1733 to march

March is the third month of the year.

1734 March

A **mare** is a female horse.

1735 mare

1732 marbles

1736 marigold

Mark the right answer.

1737 to mark

You got excellent **marks.**

1738 mark

You can buy it at the **market.**

1739 market

1740 to marry

1741 marsh

Ashley always helps to **mash** the potatoes.

1742 to mash potatoes

It is only a **mask.**

1743 mask

1744 mass

Every sailing boat has a **mast.**

1745 mast

Andrea has **mastered** the art of bicycle riding.

1746 to master

A tennis **match**

1747 match

Never play with **matches**!

1748 match

1749 mathematics

What is the **matter** with Gordon?

1750 matter

1751 mattress

May is the fifth month of the year.

1752 May

Maybe Ashley should stay at home.

The answer is not yes, and it is not no, it is **maybe**.

1753 maybe

1754 mayor

Some people call it a labyrinth.

1755 maze

Meadows are covered with grass and flowers.

1756 meadow

1757 meadowlark

1758 meal

1759 mean person

May has **measles**.

1760 measles

Measure these lines with the ruler!

1761 to measure

1762 meat

1763 mechanic

Sara won a **medal** for bravery.

1764 medal

You must be careful with **medicine**.

1765 medicine

1766 medium

Fancy **meeting** you here!

1767 to meet

The teachers are in a **meeting**.

1768   meeting

1769   melon

1770   to melt

1771   Our club has four **members**.

1772   menu

We are at the **mercy** of the weather.

The bandits showed no **mercy** to their captives.

1773   mercy

1774   mermaid

1775   merry

1776   a real **mess**

There is an important **message** on this paper.

1777   message

The **messenger** is bringing the message.

1778   messenger

A mug made of **metal**

1779   metal

Meteorites come from outer space.

1780   meteorite

1781   meter

1 **metre** = about 40 inches

1782   meter/metre*

Ashley has a **method** for learning quickly.

A **method** is a way of doing things.

There is **method** to his madness.

1783   method

A **metronome** keeps rhythm.

1784   metronome

Terry sings into the **microphone**.

1785   microphone

1786   microscope

1787   microwave oven

1788   midday

1789   in the **middle**

1790   midget

1791   midnight

One **mile** equals 1.6 kilometres.

The speed limit is 30 **miles** per hour.

1792   mile

1793   milk

1794   mill

A brilliant **mind**

$E = MC^2$

1795   mind

The **mine** is deep underground.

1796   mine

The **miner** checks the rock.

1797   miner

1798   minerals

1799   minnow

1800   mint

$7 - 5 = 2$

1801   minus

Sixty **minutes** in an hour

1802   minute

Something went wrong with this **miracle**.

1803   miracle

A **mirage** in the desert

1804   mirage

1805   mirror

Misers will not share.

1806   miser

Spud **misses** his family.

1807   I **miss** my family.

1808 missile	Michael got lost in the **mist**. **1809** mist	**1810** mistletoe	**1811** mittens
1812 to **mix**	**1813** mixer	The **moat** is full of water. **1814** moat	**1815** to **mock**
1816 mockingbird	**1817** model airplane/aeroplane*	**1818** modern chair	He should not be smiling with a **moist** nappy! **1819** moist
A **mole** on my face. **1820** mole	**1821** mole	Jane needs a **moment** to check her diary. **1822** One **moment** please.	**Monday** is the first day of the school week. Every **Monday**, Ashley gets up early. **1823** Monday
1824 money	**1825** monkey	**1826** monkfish	**1827** monster

There are 12 **months** in a year.
1828   month

A **monument** to their leader
1829   monument

1830   He is in a good **mood.**

1831   He is in a bad **mood.**

A crescent **moon**
1832   moon

1833   moose

Time to get up!
1834   morning

1835   **mortar** and pestle

1836   mosaic

1837   mosquito

Moss sometimes grows on tree trunks.
1838   moss

1839   mother

An electric **motor**
1840   motor

1841   motorcycle

A jelly **mould**
1842   mould*/mold

A **mound** of earth
1843   mound

He **mounts** his horse to go to work.
1844   to mount

1845   mountain

1846   mouse

1847   moustache*/mustache

1848 mouth

Snails **move** slowly.

1849 to **move**

Movement from side to side

1850 movement

1851 movie theater/theatre*

1852 to **mow** the lawn

1853 too **much** for me

Why is he sitting in the **mud**?

1854 mud

1855 mule

1856 to **multiply**

Being ill with **mumps** makes your face swell.

1857 mumps

To **murder** someone is an awful crime.

1858 to **murder**

1859 muscle

You can find rare things in a **museum**.

1860 museum

Some **mushrooms** are poisonous.

1861 mushroom

Ashley loves **music**.

1862 music

Ashley's Mum is a **musician**.

1863 musician

Mussels live in the sea and have hard shells.

1864 mussel

1865 You **must** jump.

1866 mustard

1867 muzzle

N

1868   nail

1869   finger**nail**

1870   **nail** clipper

What is your **name**?

1872   naked

1873   My **name** is…

1874   napkin

1871   to **nail**

A tiny **nation**!

It is healthy to eat **natural** foods.

Raisins are a **natural** source of energy.

He has not dyed his hair - that is its **natural** colour.

Nature is beautiful.

1875   too **narrow** to pass

1876   nation

1877   natural

1878   nature

Captain Jones **navigates** by the stars.

She is getting **near**.

1879   She is **naughty**.

1880   to **navigate**

1881   near

1882   neat

Bees use **nectar** to make honey.

1883   not pleasant but **necessary**

1884   neck

1885   necklace

1886   nectar

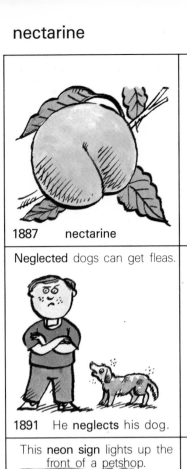

1887   nectarine

A friend in **need** is a friend indeed.

There is a great **need** for water in the desert.

1888   need

1889   I **need** water.

Can you thread a **needle**?

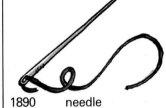

1890   needle

Neglected dogs can get fleas.

1891   He **neglects** his dog.

The horse **neighs** to wake up Ashley.

1892   to neigh

1893 neighbors/neighbours*

Neither shoe is right.

1894   **neither** one fits

This **neon sign** lights up the front of a petshop.

1895   neon sign

1896 My **nephew** is my brother's son.

There are many **nerves** in your body.

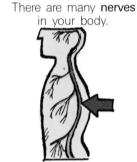

1897   nerve

Ron is so **nervous**, he never relaxes.

1898   nervous

Two eggs in the **nest**

1899   nest

Nettles can sting.

1900   nettle

Never, ever!

1901   **Never** play with fire!

1902   new

Mum reads the **news.**

The **news** is good.

Any **news** from home?

1903   news

1904   newspaper

You are **next**.

1905   Next !

The squirrel **nibbles** on a nut.

1906   to nibble

One of them is a **nice** child.

1907　nice

Nickel is a kind of metal, often used to make coins.

1908　nickel

Her name is Ashley, but her **nickname** is Spots.

1909　nickname

Ashley is Samantha's **niece**.

1910　My **niece** is my brother's daughter.

Owls hunt at **night**.

1911　night

1912　nightingale

A **nightmare** is a bad dream.

1913　nightmare

1914　nine

The answer is **NO**.

1916　no

Sir Galahad is **noble** and generous.

Helping that old lady across the street was a **noble** deed.

1917　noble

1918　nobleman

1915　ninth

There is **nobody** sitting here.

1919　There is **nobody** here.

A loud **noise**

1920　noise

Twelve o'clock **noon**

1921　noon

1922　north

There is a fly on my **nose**!

1923　nose

1924　nuts

1925　nutcracker

1926　**nylon** stockings

1927 oak

That shark must like **oars**!
1928 oar

An **oasis** in the desert
1929 oasis

An **oblong** object is longer than it is wide.
1930 oblong

1931 to observe

Ships sail across the **ocean**.
1932 ocean

An **octagon** has eight sides.
1933 octagon

The tenth month of the year
1934 October

1935 octopus

A **milometer** tells you how far you have travelled.
1936 odometer

1937 odor/odour*

Please get **off** that chair.

This food tastes **off**.

Off we go into the mountains.

The light is **off**.

1938 off

He **offers** money for the cow.
1939 to offer

1940 officer

Ashley **often** asks difficult questions.

How **often** does the train run?

Often enough!

1941 often

1942 oil

1943 ointment

A very **old** man
1944 old

Olives grow on trees.
1945 olive

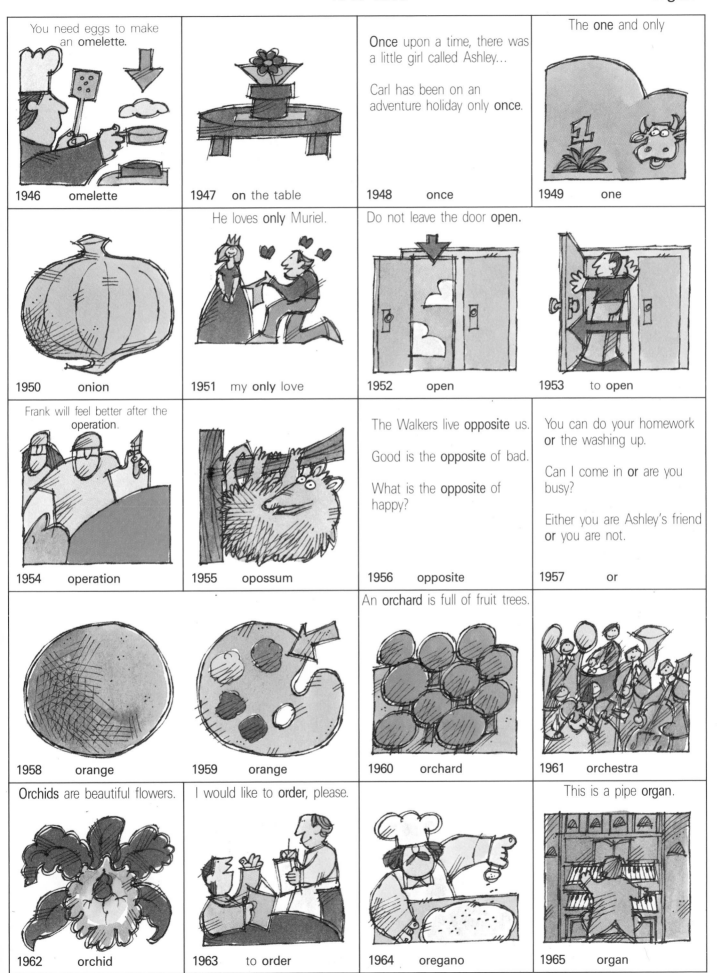

You need eggs to make an omelette.

1946   omelette

1947   on the table

Once upon a time, there was a little girl called Ashley...

Carl has been on an adventure holiday only once.

1948   once

The one and only

1949   one

1950   onion

He loves only Muriel.

1951   my only love

Do not leave the door open.

1952   open

1953   to open

Frank will feel better after the operation.

1954   operation

1955   opossum

The Walkers live opposite us.

Good is the opposite of bad.

What is the opposite of happy?

1956   opposite

You can do your homework or the washing up.

Can I come in or are you busy?

Either you are Ashley's friend or you are not.

1957   or

1958   orange

1959   orange

An orchard is full of fruit trees.

1960   orchard

1961   orchestra

Orchids are beautiful flowers.

1962   orchid

I would like to order, please.

1963   to order

1964   oregano

This is a pipe organ.

1965   organ

1966 oriole

An **orphan** has no parents.

1967 orphan

The **ostrich** cannot fly.

1968 ostrich

Otters eat fish.

1969 otter

Sixteen **ounces** to the pound

1970 ounce

The great **outdoors**

1971 outdoors

Do you like my **outfit**?

1972 outfit

1973 oval

An apple pie is baking in the **oven**.

1974 oven

Man **overboard**!

1975 Man overboard!

1976 overcoat

1977 to **overflow**

1978 overshoe

1979 to **overturn**

You **owe** respect to your teacher.

It is best not to **owe** any money.

1980 to owe

1981 owl

We **own** our house, we do not rent it.

Ashley **owns** 2 pairs of shoes.

1982 to **own**

1983 ox

1984 oxygen

This **oyster** has a pearl inside.

1985 oyster

Ashley **packs** her bag.

1986   to pack

1987   package

Someone wrote on my **pad** of paper.

1988   pad

Sharon is holding her **paddle**.

1990   paddle

1991   to paddle

1992   padlock

A launch **pad**

1989   pad

Please turn the **page**.

1993   page

A **pail** of water is very heavy.

1994   pail

1996   paint

It is not a good idea to touch **wet paint**.

1997   wet paint

Tom has hurt his finger and is in **pain**.

1995   pain

2000   painter

Aunt Polly told Tom to **paint** the fence.

1998   to paint

1999   paintbrush

2001   painting

2002   a **pair** of shoes

2003   palace

The colour of this flower is rather **pale**.

2004   pale

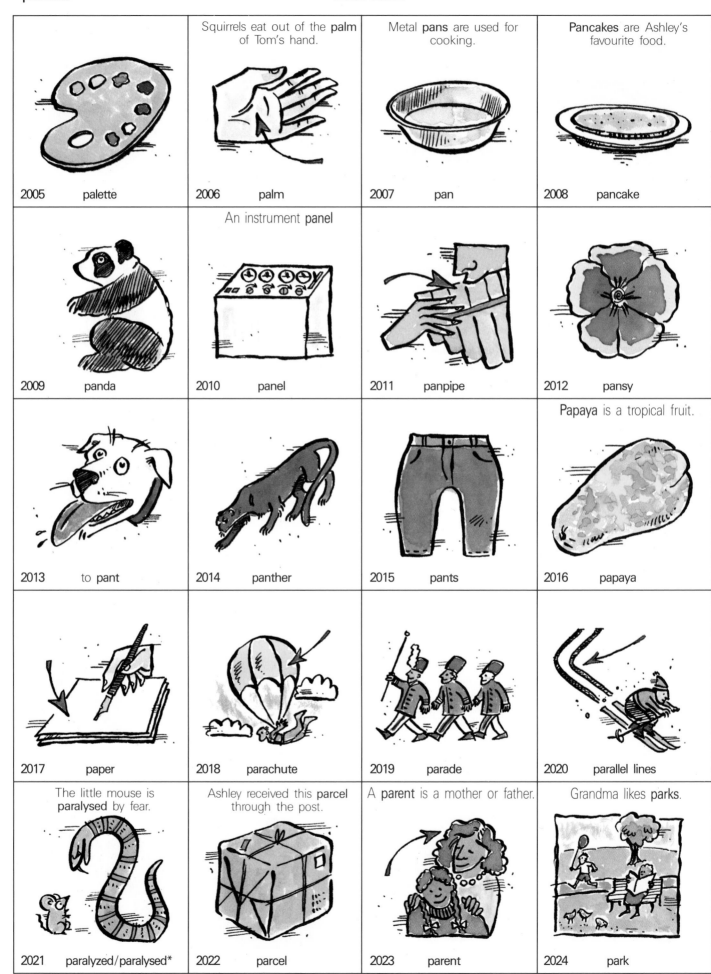

	Squirrels eat out of the **palm** of Tom's hand.	Metal **pans** are used for cooking.	**Pancakes** are Ashley's favourite food.
2005 palette	2006 palm	2007 pan	2008 pancake
2009 panda	An instrument **panel** 2010 panel	2011 panpipe	2012 pansy
2013 to pant	2014 panther	2015 pants	**Papaya** is a tropical fruit. 2016 papaya
2017 paper	2018 parachute	2019 parade	2020 parallel lines
The little mouse is **paralysed** by fear. 2021 paralyzed/paralysed*	Ashley received this **parcel** through the post. 2022 parcel	A **parent** is a mother or father. 2023 parent	Grandma likes **parks**. 2024 park

Ashley's Dad always **parks** the car here.

2025   to park

Emily's **parka** keeps her warm in winter.

2026   parka

The Houses of **Parliament**

2027   parliament

This **parrot** repeats every word you say.

2028   parrot

Parsley is a kind of herb.

2029   parsley

2030   parsnip

Dust **particles** fly in the air.

2031   particle

Charlie is a good dancing **partner**.

2032   partner

Ashley loves **parties**.

3033   party

Mary **passed** the ball...

2034   to pass

...but Joe **passed** out.

2035   to pass out

2036   passage

2037   passenger

You need a **passport** to travel abroad.

2038   passport

In the **past**, there were no planes or cars.

It is now **past** Ashley's bedtime.

Tom drove **past** our house.

2039   past

Pasta includes spaghetti and macaroni.

2040   pasta

Jim **pastes** up wallpaper.

2041   to paste

Needlework is her favourite **pastime**.

2042   pastime

Cakes and biscuits are **pastries**.

2043   pastry

Sheep graze in the **pasture**.

2044   pasture

A **patch** where it counts

2045   patch

2046   path

Ashley is not sleeping, she is waiting for her brother.

2047   She is **patient**.

One worried **patient**

2048   patient

A dress **pattern**

2049   pattern

After reading two pages, Ashley **paused** for a few seconds.

I have to **pause** for breath.

2050   to pause

2051   to step on the **pavement**

How many **paws** does a cat have?

2052   paw

Your parents have to **pay** a lot of bills.

2053   to pay

2054   pay phone

Peace on Earth

2055   peace

2056   peach

2057   peacock

2058   peak

2059   peal of a bell

2060   peanut

2061   pear

A **pearl** in the oyster

2062   pearl

Peas in a pod

2063   peas

Peat moss helps plants grow.

2064   peat moss

Pebbles on the beach

2065   pebbles

A pecan is a nut.

2066   pecan

2067   to peck

2068   pedal

2070   pedestrian

It is safer to cross the road at a zebra crossing.

2071   pedestrian crossing

2072   to peel

2069   to pedal

2073   pelican

2074   pen

2075   pencil

A pendulum clock

2076   pendulum

2077   penguin

The blade of a penknife folds away when not in use.

2078   penknife

A pentagon has five sides.

2079   pentagon

Many happy people

2080   people

A pepper mill

2081   pepper

2082   peppermint

2083   perch

A bird on its perch

2084   perch

A great **performance**

2085 performance

2086 perfume

The **full stop** comes at the end of a sentence.

glurg!

2087 period

2088 periwinkle

Tom is a young male **person**.

2089 person

2090 pest

Burt **pesters** his dad.

2091 to pester

My **pet** snake

2092 pet

Flowers have **petals**.

2094 petal

2095 petunia

The hospital **pharmacist** makes up the prescripton.

2096 pharmacist

The baby **pets** the dog.

2093 to pet

2097 pharmacy

2098 pheasant

Phone or telephone

2099 phone

2100 photograph

2101 piano

Pick a card!

2102 to pick

Emily **picks up** the doll.

2103 to pick up

2104 pickaxe

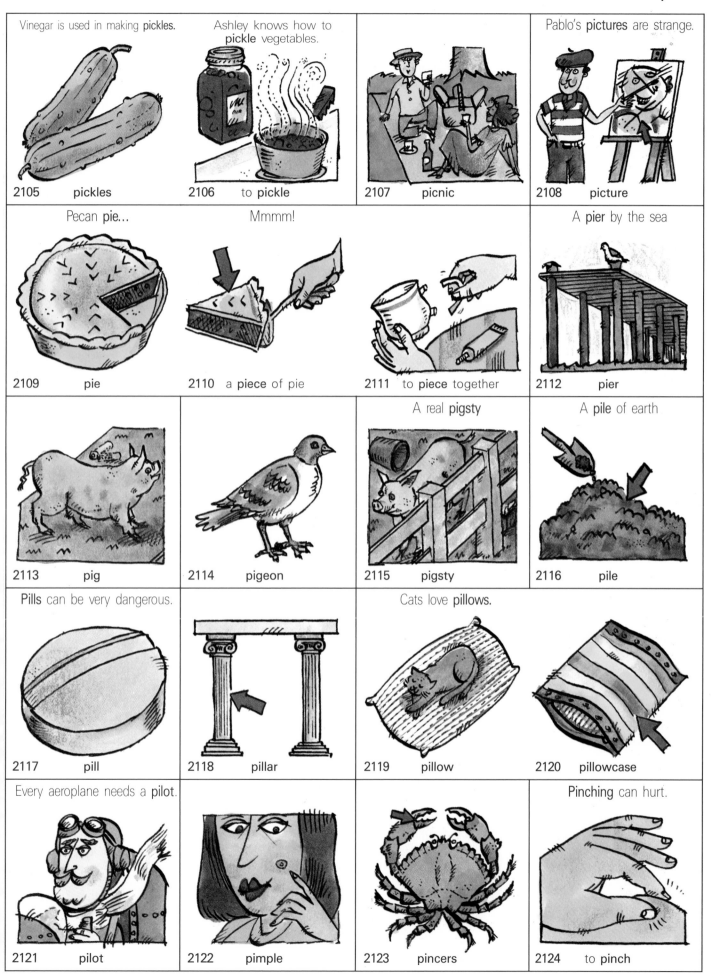

Vinegar is used in making **pickles.**

2105   pickles

Ashley knows how to **pickle** vegetables.

2106   to **pickle**

2107   picnic

Pablo's **pictures** are strange.

2108   picture

Pecan **pie...**   Mmmm!

2109   pie

2110   a **piece** of pie

2111   to **piece** together

A **pier** by the sea

2112   pier

2113   pig

2114   pigeon

A real **pigsty**

2115   pigsty

A **pile** of earth

2116   pile

Pills can be very dangerous.

2117   pill

2118   pillar

Cats love **pillows.**

2119   pillow

2120   pillowcase

Every aeroplane needs a **pilot.**

2121   pilot

2122   pimple

2123   pincers

Pinching can hurt.

2124   to **pinch**

Pineapples do not grow
on pine trees.

2125   pine

2126   pineapple

2127   pink

2128   pipe

2129   pirate

2130   pistachio

A very old **pistol**

2131   pistol

Merv **pitches** the baseball.

2132   to pitch

Ashley **pities** the poor boy
who lost his cat.

What a **pity** ....

2136   to pity

There is no **place** like home.

Would you like to come to
our **place**?

Try to keep everything
in **place**!

2137   place

2138   plaice

Hey Merv, that was a good
pitch!

This song is off **pitch**.

Salesmen like to make a
pitch.

2133   pitch

2139   plain shirt

The **plain** stretches for
hundreds of miles.

2140   plain

2141   to plan

2134   pitchfork

This **plane** belongs
to a carpenter.

2142   plane

Planets around the sun

2143   planets

2144   plank

2135   pitch tar

2145   plants

2146   to plant

Pam **plasters** the wall.

2147   plaster

2148   to plaster

Many household objects are made of **plastic**.

2149   plastic

2150   plasticine

This is Ashley's dinner **plate**.

2151   plate

2152   plateau

The train is at the **platform**.

2153   platform

Children **play** together in the **playground**.

2154   to play

2155   playground

2156   playing cards

Please spare my life, I beg of you!

2157   to plead

2158   a pleasant day

2159 A glass of milk **please**.

This kilt has many **pleats**.

2160   pleat

2161   pliers

2162   plow/plough*

2163   to pluck

2164   plug

2165 plug	2166 plum	2167 plumber	2168 plump
'One' is singular, 'many' is **plural**. Children is the **plural** of child. 2169 plural	One **plus** one equals… 2170 plus	2171 plywood	Jacques **poaches** some eggs. 2172 to poach
2173 pocket	2174 pea pod	A **poem** has sets of words that rhyme, A poet writes **poems** and has a good time. 2175 poem	It is not polite to **point**. 2177 to point
2176 poinsettia	2180 poison	Some insects have a **poisonous** sting. There are not many **poisonous** snakes. 2181 poisonous	A very sharp **point** 2178 point
If you **poke** me in the back, I get very cross. 2182 to poke	2183 polar bear	2184 pole	2179 pointed

2185 policeman

2186 policewoman

Henry **polishes** the cup until it shines.

2187 to polish

Everybody likes **polite** children.

It is not **polite** to shout.

The teacher expects a **polite** answer.

2188 polite

Pollen gives some people hayfever.

2189 pollen

2190 pomegranate

2191 pond

Susie rides her **pony** every morning.

2192 pony

Fun at the swimming **pool**

2193 pool

We **pool** our resources.

2194 to pool

Ashley had **poor** results because she did not work hard.

Her family is not **poor**, but it is not rich either.

2195 poor

2196 to pop

2197 poplar

2198 poppy

Ashley is a **popular** girl.

This book is very **popular.**

2199 popular

Ron sits on the **porch.**

2200 porch

2201 **Pores** are little holes in the skin.

Porridge for breakfast

2202 porridge

2203 port

Ashley wants a **portable** radio, but she has not saved up enough money from her allowance.

Susie watches her **portable** TV in the garden.

2204 portable

The **porter** carries Aunt Vera's luggage.

2205   porter

This is a **portrait** of Aunt Vera.

2206   portrait

2207   post

Peter **posts** a letter to Aunt Vera.

2208   to **post**

Aunt Vera sends a **postcard** to Peter.

2210   postcard

2211   poster

2212   pot

2209   post office

2213   potato

2214   pottery

Do you keep your coins in a **pouch**?

2215   pouch

2216   to **pounce**

Four bananas weigh about a **pound**.

One **pound** is quite a lot of money in England.

2217   pound

2218   to **pound**

2219   to **pour**

2220   to **pout**

Eric puts on talcum **powder** after his bath.

2221   powder

2222   to practice/practise*

Wheat grows on the **prairies**.

2223   prairie

Good show, children!

2224   to praise

The horse **prances** about.

2225   to prance

2226   to pray

I **prefer** that one.

2227   to prefer

Her baby is expected next month.

2228   She is **pregnant**.

2229   I am **present**.

2230   birthday **present**

Bob **presents** the trophy.

2231   to present

2232   fruit **preserves**

Press the button to call the lift.

2233   to press

2234   pretty

The owl caught its **prey**.

2235   prey

2236   price

2237   to prick

2238   prickly animal

2239   primary school

2240   primrose

2241   prince

2242   princess

2243   school principal

In **principle**, I agree with you.

The first **principle** is hard work.

Truth is a sacred **principle**.

2244   principle

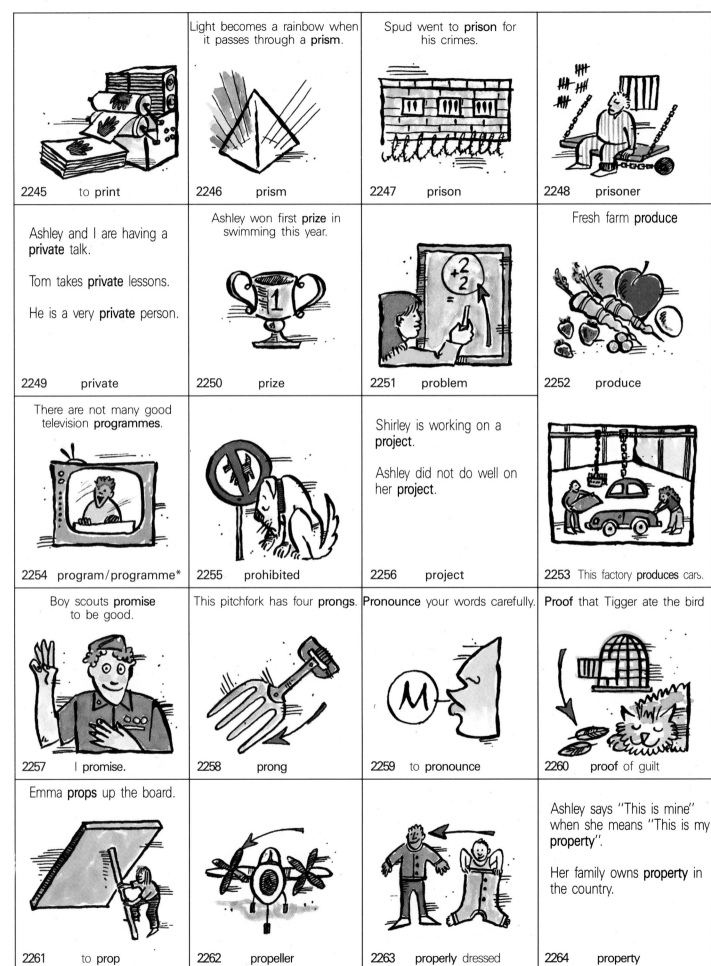

2245   to print

Light becomes a rainbow when it passes through a **prism**.

2246   prism

Spud went to **prison** for his crimes.

2247   prison

2248   prisoner

Ashley and I are having a **private** talk.

Tom takes **private** lessons.

He is a very **private** person.

2249   private

Ashley won first **prize** in swimming this year.

2250   prize

2251   problem

Fresh farm **produce**

2252   produce

There are not many good television **programmes**.

2254   program/programme*

2255   prohibited

Shirley is working on a **project**.

Ashley did not do well on her **project**.

2256   project

2253   This factory **produces** cars.

Boy scouts **promise** to be good.

2257   I promise.

This pitchfork has four **prongs**.

2258   prong

Pronounce your words carefully.

2259   to pronounce

Proof that Tigger ate the bird

2260   proof of guilt

Emma **props** up the board.

2261   to prop

2262   propeller

2263   properly dressed

Ashley says "This is mine" when she means "This is my **property**".

Her family owns **property** in the country.

2264   property

2265   to **protest**

2266   I am a **proud** cat.

I can **prove** it, Sir.

2267   to **prove**

Here is a **proverb**:

"An apple a day keeps the doctor away."

2268   **proverb**

2269   to **provide** chairs

A **prune** is a dried plum.

2270   **prune**

2271   to **prune**

2272   **public** telephone

Pudding for dessert

2273   **pudding**

2274   **puddle**

2275   to **puff**

2276   **puffin**

2277   to **pull**

2278   **pulley**

2279   **pullover**

The doctor takes Ashley's **pulse**.

2280   **pulse**

2281   **pump**

2282   to **pump**

2283   **pumpkin**

2284   to **punch**

You have arrived on time.

2285   You are **punctual**.

Tom will be punished for **puncturing** the tyre.

2286   to **puncture**

2287   to **punish**

2288   **punishment**

A **puppet** like Pinocchio

2289   **puppet**

2290   **puppy**

2291   **pure** water

2292   **purple**

Cats **purr** when they are happy.

2293   to **purr**

2294   **purse**

2295   to **pursue**

2296   to **push**

Put it here, please.

2297   to **put**

2298   to **put away**

Tim **puts off** reading until later.

2299   to **put off**

Putty keeps the window pane in place.

2300   **putty**

2301   **puzzle**

2302   **pyjamas***/**pajamas**

2303   **pyramid**

2304   **python**

2305 quail

2306 **quality** watch

Ashley says "amount" when she means "**quantity**".

2307 quantity

2308 to quarrel

There are stone **quarries** and sand **quarries**.

2309 quarry

2310 quarter

A boat docked at the **quay**.

2311 quay

2312 queen

2313 to ask a **question**

Be **quick** about it!

2314 quick

He is sinking in **quicksand**.

2315 quicksand

2316 She is **quiet**.

A **quill** is a feather used as a pen.

2317 quill

2318 porcupine **quill**

2319 quilt/eiderdown*

2320 quince

A **quiver** full of arrows

2321 quiver

2322 to quiver

Our class had a **quiz** in spelling today.

2323 quiz

R

2324 rabbit

2325 raccoon

2326 to race

2327 rack

Terry makes a **racket**.

2328 racket

2329 radiator

2330 radio

2331 radish

The **radius** of a circle

2332 radius

2333 raft

2334 a **raid** in progress

Hold on to the hand**rail**.

2335 hand**rail**

2336 railroad track

It is **raining** cats and dogs.

2337 to rain

Ashley loves to watch **rainbows**.

2338 rainbow

2339 raincoat

All those who like Ashley, **raise** your hands!

She has **raised** an interesting question.

2340 to raise

Raisins are dried grapes.

2341 raisin

2342 rake

Billy **raps** on the door.

2343 to rap

2344 rapid

2345 rare

A **rash** on his face

2346 rash

2347 raspberry

2348 rat

2349 rattle

2350 rattlesnake

2351 raven

2352 ravenous

2353 ravine

2354 a **raw** egg

2355 **ray** of sunlight

2356 razor

2357 to reach

2358 to read

On your marks...**ready**...

2359 ready

Is this a **real** diamond?

2360 real

2361 to realize

Kathy is **really** happy.

2362 Are you **really** here?

2363 rear

2364 rearview mirror

John tries to **reason** with the examiner.

2365 to reason

That is a **reasonable** price.

Ashley, please be **reasonable**.

2366 reasonable

People do **rebel** against high taxes.

Spartacus **rebelled** against Rome.

2367 to rebel

2368 I do not **recall**.

Sally has just **received** a gift.

2369 to receive

2370 **recently** hatched

2371 recipe

Can you **recite** a poem?

2372 to recite

2373 record

2374 record player

Ashley scraped her knee but she will **recover** quickly.

I **recovered** all the books that were left outside.

2375 to recover

2376 rectangle

2377 red

2378 reed

A coral **reef**

2379 reef

Something in there really **reeks**.

2380 to reek

The line is wound on the **reel**.

2381 reel

2382 referee

2383   reflection

Never leave the **refrigerator** door open.

2384   refrigerator

2385   to refuse

This **region** of the country is crossed by rivers.

2386   region

2387   to register

Tom **regrets** what happened.

2388   to regret

2389   Actors **rehearse** a play.

2390   reindeer

2391   reins

2392   relatives

2393   to relax

2394   to release

2395   **Remember** to brush your teeth.

2396   remote island

Phil **removes** his hat.

2397   to remove

We **rent** a flat.

If you do not have a car, you can **rent** one.

2398   to rent

2399   to repair

The parrot **repeats** every word.

2400   to repeat

2401   to replace

He asked and she **replied**.

2402   to reply

2403 reptile

Jim **rescues** the cat.

2404 to rescue

Water is stored in a **reservoir.**

2405 reservoir

Ashley, you are **responsible** for your little brother Carl.

Dad saw the milk spilled on the floor and said:"Who is **responsible** for this?"

2406 responsible

2407 to rest

2408 restaurant

Ashley always **returns** her library books.

John is away from home, but he will **return** soon.

2409 to return

2410 reverse

2411 rhinoceros

2412 rhubarb

Here is a **rhyme** for you:

Hickory dickory dock,
The mouse ran up the clock.
The clock struck one,
The mouse ran down,
Hickory dickory dock.

2413 rhyme

2414 rib

Can you make a bow with **ribbon**?

2415 ribbon

A bowl of **rice**

2416 rice

The ribbon is a **rich** red colour.

The **rich** must always help the poor.

2417 rich

Nobody can solve this **riddle.**

2418 riddle

2419 to **ride** a horse

2420 ridge

2421 my **right** hand

Turn **right** at the corner.

It is not **right** to steal.

Ashley thinks she is always **right**.

Hold it the **right** way up.

2422 right

2423   right-handed

The sausage has a tough **rind**.

2424   rind

2425   ring

Uncle Sam **rings** the doorbell.

2426   to ring

An ice hockey **rink**

2427   rink

Ashley's dad **rinses** the dishes.

2428   to rinse

2429   riot

You must have **ripped** your trousers!

2430   to rip

This apple is **ready** to eat.

2431   ripe

2432   ripple

2433   The sun **rises**.

Always be careful when taking **risks**.

The weather forecaster said there was a **risk** of frost.

2434   risk

2435   rivals

2436   river

2437   road

The lion **roars** to impress Mr. Tamer.

2438   to roar

A nice **roast** straight from the oven.

2439   roast

Robbers are criminals.

2440   robber

2441   robin

2442   rock

2443 to **rock**	2444 **rocket**	2445 **rocking** chair	2446 **rod**
2447 **roll**	2448 to **roll**	2449 **roller** skate	2450 **rolling** pin
Our house has a tile **roof**. 2451 **roof**	2452 **room**	Hens **roost** at night. 2453 to **roost**	2454 **root**
2455 **rope**	2456 **rose**	2457 **rosemary**	Karen has **rosy** cheeks. 2458 **rosy**
2459 **rotten** apple	A rather **rough** beard 2460 **rough**	2461 **round**	2462 4 buttons in a **row**

She **rows** faster than Michael.

2463   to **row**

The king is part of the **royal** family.

2464   **royal**

Tyres and balls are made of **rubber**.

2465   **rubber**

2466   **rubbish**

2467   **ruby**

A **rudder** is used for steering.

2468   **rudder**

2469   He is **rude**.

This is difficult country to walk through.

2470   **rugged** terrain

The **ruins** of an ancient castle

2471   **ruin**

Some countries are under the **rule** of a king.

Ashley seldom breaks the **rules**.

Mum and Dad make the **rules** in this house.

2472   **rule**

The king is the **ruler**.

2473   **ruler**

2474   I hear a **rumble**.

Can he **run** faster than a speeding bullet?

2475   to **run**

2476   to **run away**

2477   to **run over**

2478   to **run out** of energy

She **rushed** to catch it, but it was too late.

2479   to **rush**

Iron man has **rust** everywhere.

2480   **rust**

The car is stuck in a **rut**.

2481   **rut**

2482   **rye**

A **sack** of flour

2483   sack

2484   Truth is a **sacred** principle.

2485   sad

2486   saddle

What is inside the **safe**?

2487   safe

2488   sail

2489   sailboard

2490   sailboat

2491   sailor

2492   salad

It is going cheap in the **sale**.

2493   sale

2494   salmon

Salt and pepper

2495   salt

2496   to salute

2497   same

2498   sand

2499   sandal

Ashley can make her own **sandwich**.

2500   sandwich

2501   sap

Many **sardines** in a can

2502   sardine

We receive TV pictures by **satellite**.

2503   satellite

Satin is smooth and shiny.

2504   satin dress

The weekend starts on **Saturday**.

Saturday is play day.

Ashley likes **Saturdays**.

2505   Saturday

2506   sauce

2507   sausage

2508   I **save** my money.

This **saw** is very sharp.

2509   saw

2511   sawdust

2512   I **say** what I think.

The **scaffolding** supports the artist.

2513   scaffolding

2510   to saw

Careful not to **scald** yourself!

2514   to scald

One side is heavier.

2515   scale

Scallops are very tasty.

2516   scallop

2517   scalp

The man with the **scar**

2518   scar

She likes to **scare** him.

2519   to **scare**

Scarecrows are for the birds.

2520   scarecrow

A very warm **scarf**

2521   scarf

2522   scarlet

The police are at the **scene**.

2523   **scene** of a crime

2524   scenery

Scholarship means learning.

2525   scholarship

This is the **school** Ashley goes to.

2526   school

2527   schooner

2528   scissors

2529   to scoop

2530   scooter

The paper is not quite burnt.

2531   scorched paper

2532   to score

2533   scout

2534   scraps of paper

I always **scrape** my knees.

2535   scrape

2536   scraper

2537   scratch

2538   screen

2539   screw

2540   screwdriver

Wally **scrubs** the floor.

2541   to scrub

2542   sculptor

2543   seahorse

There is a lot of water in the sea.
2544   Adriatic sea

2545   seagull

2546   seal

2547   seam

What is Harry looking for?
2548   to search

2549   searchlight

The four seasons are:
Spring
Summer
Autumn
Winter
2550   seasons

2551   seat

Ashley has fastened her seatbelt.
2552   seatbelt

2553   seaweed

2554   second

Ashley knows how to keep a secret.
2555   I have a secret.

2556   to see

2557   see-saw

The seed grows into a new plant.
2558   seed

Later, the bird revived.
2559   It seems dead.

2560   to seize

Ashley does not like selfish kids.
2561   You are selfish.

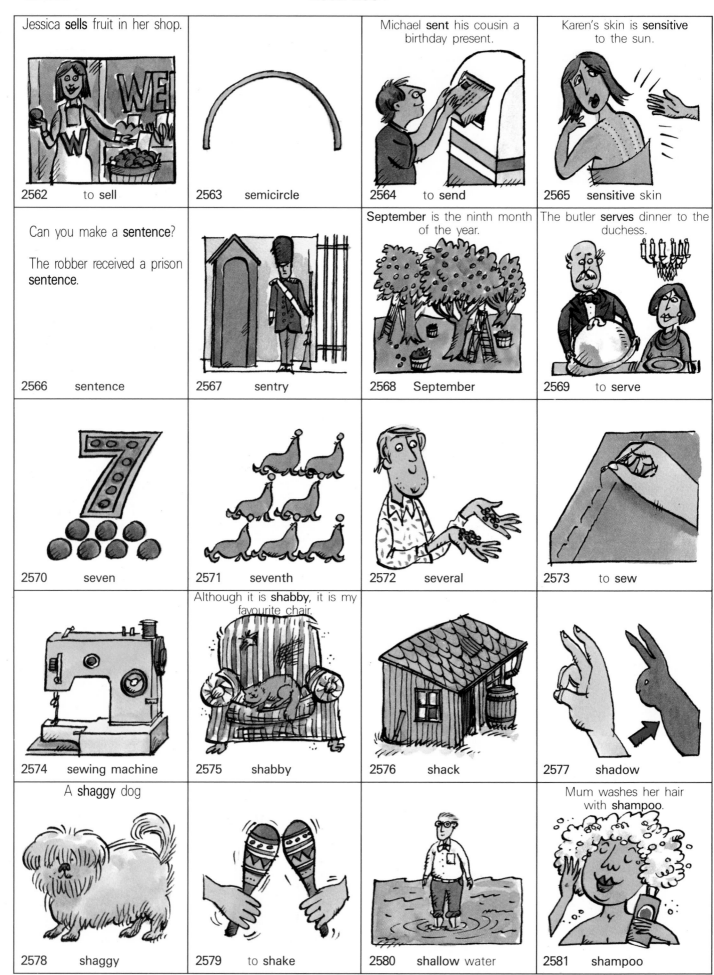

Jessica **sells** fruit in her shop.

2562   to **sell**

2563   **semicircle**

Michael **sent** his cousin a birthday present.

2564   to **send**

Karen's skin is **sensitive** to the sun.

2565   **sensitive** skin

Can you make a **sentence**?

The robber received a prison **sentence**.

2566   **sentence**

2567   **sentry**

September is the ninth month of the year.

2568   **September**

The butler **serves** dinner to the duchess.

2569   to **serve**

2570   **seven**

2571   **seventh**

2572   **several**

2573   to **sew**

2574   **sewing** machine

Although it is **shabby**, it is my favourite chair.

2575   **shabby**

2576   **shack**

2577   **shadow**

A **shaggy** dog

2578   **shaggy**

2579   to **shake**

2580   **shallow** water

Mum washes her hair with **shampoo**.

2581   **shampoo**

We can **share** it.

2582   to share

Is this **shark** learning how to fly?

2583   shark

2584   sharp

2585   knife sharpener

The glass **shattered**.

2588   to shatter

2589   to shave

2590   shears

2586   skate sharpener

2591   sheath

Ashley counts **sheep** before falling asleep.

2592   sheep

Tuck in the **sheet** when you make the bed.

2593   sheet

2587   pencil sharpener

2594   shelf

2595   shell

The leaf is the beetle's **shelter**.

2596   shelter

2597   shepherd

2598   shield

2599   shin

The sun **shines** brightly.

2600   to shine

2601   shingle

Shingles is a disease.

2602   shingles

2603   shiny

2604   ship

2605   shipwreck

2606   shirt

2607   to shiver

Avoid electric **shocks**!

2608   shock

2609   shoes

2610   shoelace

2611   shoemaker

2612   to shoot

2613   shop

2614   shopkeeper

2615   shop window

The water starts at the **shore**.

2616   shore

2617   short

2618   shorts

2619   shoulder

2620   to shout

It is very rude to **shove** people.

2621   to shove

A snow **shovel**

2622   shovel

2623   to **show**

2624   to **show off**

2625   He finally **showed up.**

Curtis takes a **shower.**

2626   shower

2627   to **shriek**

2628   shrimp

2629   to **shrink**

2630   shrub

Mr. Fast **shuffles** the cards.

2631   shuffle

The **shutters** are closed at night.

2632   shutters

2633   shy

2634   sick

There are no windows on this **side.**

2635   side

Always walk on the **pavement.**

2636   sidewalk

A heavy **sigh**

2637   to **sigh**

2638   sign

2639   to **signal**

2640   signature

Ashley is not **silent** very often.

A **silent** night is a quiet night.

2641   silent

The window **sill**

2642   sill

Jonathan thinks Ashley is **silly**.

Ashley thinks Jonathan does **silly** things.

2643   silly

Silver is a precious metal.

2644   silver

That is the truth, pure and **simple**.

There is a **simple** solution.

2645   simple

2646   to sing

'One' is **singular**.

'Several' is plural.

2647   singular

2648   sink

Sink or swim!

2649   to sink

Marg is **sipping** her drink.

2650   to sip

2651   siren

My **sister** and I have the same parents.

2652   sister

2653   to sit

2654   six

2655   sixth

Does it come in my **size**?

2656   size

2657   to skate

2658   skateboard

What is a **skeleton** doing in my cupboard?

2659   skeleton

2660   to sketch

2661   skis

2662 to ski	Horace almost **skidded** off the path. 2663 to skid	2664 skin	2665 to skip
2666 skipper	2667 skirt	2668 skull	There are clouds in the **sky**. 2669 sky
2670 skylark	A **skyscraper** is a very tall building. 2671 skyscraper	He **slammed** the door. 2672 to slam	2673 slanted floor
2674 to slap	Zorro is **slashing** around again. 2675 to slash	Paul writes on the **slate** with chalk. 2676 slate	2677 sled
Zorro is **sleeping**. 2678 to sleep	A **sleeping bag** for camping. 2679 sleeping bag	Paul feels **sleepy**. 2680 sleepy	I wish this **sleet** would turn to proper snow. 2681 sleet

2682   sleeve

2683   slide

2684   slim

A **slimy** creature

2685   slimy

His arm is in a **sling**.

2686   sling

2687   slingshot

2688   to slip

2689   slipper

2690   slippery

What a **slob**!

2691   slob

2692   slope

2693   slot

You must not **slouch**.

2694   to slouch

The car **slows down** at the corner.

Slow down, Dad! You are going too fast.

Nothing can **slow** Ashley **down**.

2695   to slow down

2696   slush

2697   small

That was a **smart** thing to do.

She is wearing a **smart** dress.

2698   smart

Do not **smash** the watch!

2699   to smash

2700   to smear

Hector **smells** the flower.

2701   to smell

What a **smelly** skunk!

2702   smelly

People who **smoke** are like skunks.

2703   to smoke

The ice Ashley is skating on is very **smooth**.

A good aeroplane pilot makes **smooth** landings.

2704   smooth

2705   to snack

2706   snail

2707   snake

2708   to snap

2709   sneakers

The dust made her **sneeze**.

2710   to sneeze

2711   snorkel

2712   snow

2713   snowflake

2714   snowshoes

Wash with **soap** and water!

2715   soap

They call it **soccer** in America but football in England.

2716   soccer

2717   sock

2718   socket

2719   sofa

Soft and cuddly

2720   soft

2721   soldier

2722 sole	2723 She **solves** the problem.	2724 to **somersault**	2725 son

2726   song

Soon it will be dark.

Ashley will be home **soon**.

She **soon** got tired of her new doll.

2727   soon

2728   sorcerer

2729   My arm is **sore**.

Sorrel is very tasty.

2730   sorrel

Grover is truly **sorry**.

2731   sorry

2732   to **sort**

2733   soup

2734   sour

2735   south

The **sow** is the mother of the piglets.

2736   sow

The farmer **sows** the seed on the field.

2737   to **sow**

2738   spaceship

2739   spade

2740   to **spank**

Every car must have a **spare** tyre.

2741   spare tire/tyre*

	Her rings **sparkle** in the sun.		They both **speak** English.
2742 spark	2743 to sparkle	2744 sparrow	2745 to speak
	The turtle is slow even when it **speeds up**.	Alice is about to **spell** her name.	
2746 spear	2747 to speed up	2748 to spell	2749 to spend
A **sphere** is round.	Hot and **spicy**	The **spider** spins a web.	
2750 sphere	2751 spicy	2752 spider	2753 spike
		Spinach is one of my favourite vegetables.	Also called the backbone
2754 to spill	2755 to spin	2756 spinach	2757 spine
		No polite person ever **spits**.	
2758 spiral	2759 spire	2760 to spit	2761 to splash

There are **splinters** everywhere.

2762   splinter

2763   **spoiled** fruit

2764   sponge

2765   **spool** of thread

2766   spoon

How did that **spot** get there?

2767   spot

2768   spout

Ashley **sprained** her ankle.

2769   to sprain

2770   to spray

2771   to spread

2772   spring

Spring is here at last.

2773   spring

2775   to sprinkle

She **sprints** to win.

2776   to sprint

2777   spruce

The **spring** runs swiftly.

2774   spring

2778   square

2779   squash

2780   to squat

Ashley **squeezes** and hugs her friend.

2781   to squeeze

2782   squid

2783   squirrel

2784   to squirt

The horses are in the **stable**.

2785   stable

A dancer on **stage**

2786   stage

2787   stain

2788   staircase

2789   wooden stake

Stale bread is dry and hard.

2790   stale bread

2791   celery stalk

A **stallion** is a male horse.

2792   stallion

2793   stamp

2794   to stand

Twinkle, twinkle little **star**!

2795   star

Ashley is **staring** at you.

2796   to stare

2797   starling

2798   to start a car

When Ashley says "I'm **starving**", she means that she is hungry.

You will not **starve**, Ashley!

2799   to starve

2800   gas station

2801   train station

2802   statue

2803   Stay there!

Steak is a cut of meat.
2804   steak

2805   to steal

2806   steam

2807   Knives are made of steel.

2808   steep

2809   steer

2811   stem

2812   step

She stepped in the puddle.
2813   to step in

2810   to steer

Dad made stew for dinner.
2815   stew

2816   stick

2814 to step out for a minute

Bud's hands are all sticky.
2817   sticky

Uncle Joe has a stiff leg.

Can you keep a stiff upper lip?

2818   stiff

It really stings.
2819   to sting

A bee sting
2820   sting

Skunks stink.
2821   to stink

Stir it before you taste it!

2822   to **stir**

2823   **stockings**

2824   to **stoke**

2825   **stomach**

Throwing **stones** is dangerous.

2826   **stone**

The spider will land on the **stool**.

2827   **stool**

She **stoops** to get the ball.

2828   to **stoop**

2829   **stop**

2832   **store**

Is this the **stork** that brought Ashley?

2833   **stork**

2834   **storm**

2830   He **stops** the train.

Aunt Sally reads a **story**.

2835   **story**

2836   **stove**

2837   **straight**

2831   **stop-over**

2838   to **strain**

2839   to **strain**

A very **strange** animal

2840   **strange**

Jim got too close and the ape is **strangling** him.

2841   to **strangle**

2842 strap	2843 straw	2844 strawberry	2845 stream
2846 streamer	2847 street	2848 street light	How far can she **stretch** it? 2849 to stretch
2850 stretcher	The workers are on **strike** for more money. 2851 strike	It is not nice to **strike** people. 2852 to strike	2853 string
Lots of **stripes** 2854 stripe	2855 strong	2856 student	2857 to study
2858 a **stuffed** animal	2859 stump	A **submarine** travels underwater. 2860 submarine	2861 to subtract

2862 to suck	**Suddenly,** it began to rain. Pamela left **suddenly**. 2863 suddenly	Too much **sugar** is bad for you. 2864 sugar	2865 suit
2866 suitcase	2867 summer	2868 sun	**Sunday** is the day between Saturday and Monday. 2869 Sunday
The **sundial** tells the time. 2870 sundial	The **sunflower** always faces the sun. 2871 sunflower	2872 sunrise	2873 sunset
We shop at the **supermarket**. 2874 supermarket	2875 supper	I am **sure** tomorrow will be a sunny day. Ashley will go tomorrow for **sure**. That is a **sure** way to win. 2876 sure	The **surface** of the moon is pitted with craters. 2877 surface
2878 surgeon	My first name is Ashley and my **surname** is Potter. 2879 surname	They didn't tell Ashley beforehand. 2880 surprise party	I give myself up! 2881 to surrender

They have **surrounded** him.

2882   to **surround**

2883   **suspenders**

2884   to **swallow**

2885   **swan**

2886   to **swap**

A **swarm** of angry bees

2887   **swarm**

It gets very hot in the sauna.

2888   to **sweat**

2889   **sweater**

2890   to **sweep**

2891   **sweet**

The car **swerved** to miss the cat.

2892   to **swerve**

Gerry can **swim** like a fish.

2893   to **swim**

2894   **swing**

2895   to **swing**

2896   **switch**

Switch on the light, please.

It is best to **switch** off the television.

2897   to **switch**

2898   to **swoop**

2899   **sword**

2900   **sycamore**

Pancakes and maple **syrup**

2901   **syrup**

The mug is on the **table**.

2902 table

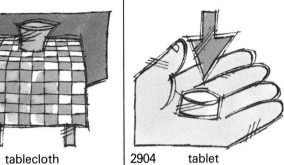

2903 tablecloth

2904 tablet

2905 tack

Ashley must **tackle** that problem soon.

Al **tackled** Hector during the football game.

2906 to tackle

Tadpoles become frogs.

2907 tadpole

2908 tail

2910 to take

2911 to take apart

2912 to take away

2913 to take back

2914 to take off

2915 to take off

2916 to take out

2917 take-out

2909 tailor

Sylvia tells a long **tale** to Ashley

2918 tale

Ashley and Sylvia are in the **talent** show.

Sylvia has a great **talent** for acting.

2919 talent

It is Ashley's turn to **talk**.

2920 to talk

2921 tall	2922 tambourine	Circus lions are **tame**. 2923 tame	2924 tan
2925 tangerine	2926 tangled	2927 tank	2928 tanker
This **tap** drips. 2929 tap	2930 tape	2931 to tape	2932 tape recorder
2933 tar	2934 target	2935 tarragon	2936 tart
His **task** is to sweep the floor. 2937 task	2938 to taste	This is very **tasty** food, I am enjoying it a lot. 2939 tasty	2940 taxicab

	Miss Parker **teaches** us at school.	She is our **teacher**.	All on the same **team**
2941 a cup of **tea**	2942 to **teach**	2943 **teacher**	2944 **team**

2945   **tea**pot | 2946   **tear** | 2947   to **tear** | Never **tear out** a page! / 2948   to **tear out**

This **telegram** contains urgent news.

2949   **telegram** | 2950   **telephone** | 2951   to **telephone** | 2952   **telescope**

Also called **telly** for short | Guess what I heard! | Grover has a bad **temper**. He cannot control his **temper**. |

2953   **television** | 2954   to **tell** | 2955   **temper** | 2956   **temperature**

2957   **ten** apples | 2958   **tennis** racquet and ball | 2959   **tennis** shoe | Ashley has slept in a **tent**. / 2960   **tent**

2961　tenth	A computer **terminal** 2962　terminal	2963　to **test** the water	2964　to **thank**
The ground **thaws** in the spring. 2965　to **thaw**	2966　theater/theatre*	2967　there	2968　thermometer
2969　thick	A **thief** is also called a robber. 2970　thief	2971　thigh	2972　thimble
2973　thin	A person is not a **thing**. Ashley says many funny **things**. 2974　thing	2975　to **think**	2976　third
2977　thirsty	2978　thistle	**Thorns** can hurt. 2979　thorn	2980　thread

Ashley can only **thread** a large needle.

2981   to **thread**

2982   **three**

2983   **threshold**

2984   **throat**

The **throne** of the Queen

2985   **throne**

2986   to **throw**

2987   to **throw up**

2988   **thumb**

A loud clap of **thunder**

2989   **thunder**

2990   **thunderstorm**

Thursday is the fifth day of the week.

Ashley goes to her swimming lesson on **Thursdays**.

2991   **Thursday**

2992   **thyme**

2993   **ticket**

2994   to **tickle**

At least one of them is **tidy**!

2995   **tidy**

I can fasten my own **tie**.

2996   **tie**

2998   **tiger**

2999   to **tighten**

3000   **tiles**

2997   to **tie**

The boat is **tilting** dangerously.

3001   to tilt

3002   What time is it?

3003   tiny

The boat has **tipped** over.

3004   to tip

3006   to tiptoe

Our car needs new **tyres**.

3007   tire/tyre*

3008   tired

3005   to tip

3009   toad

Toast and jam

3010   toast

3011   toaster

School starts **today**.

Today is Mothers' Day.

Do your homework **today**!

3012   today

3013   toes

3014   We are sitting **together**.

3015   toilet

3016   tomato

Someone is buried in this **tomb**.

3017   tomb

Tomorrow is another day.

Ashley is going to see the dinosaurs at the museum **tomorrow**.

3018   tomorrow

3019   tongs

It is very rude to stick out your **tongue**.

3020   tongue

3021 It weighs a **ton**.	3022 tonsils	3023 tools	3024 tooth
3025 toothache	3026 toothbrush	3027 toothpaste	3028 top

The blocks **toppled** over.

The Olympic **torch**

The **top** is spinning.

| 3030   to **topple** | 3031   torch | 3032   tornado | 3029   top |

After the storm, the river flowed in a **torrent**.

Cal **tosses** the ball to Sue.

| 3033   torrent | 3034   tortoise | 3035   to **toss** | 3036   to **touch** |

Ashley's **towel** is wet.

The world's tallest **tower**

| 3037   I am **tough**. | 3038   to **tow** | 3039   towel | 3040   tower |

3041   town

This **town** is near Ashley's home.

3042   toys

Pick up your **toys**, please!

3043   to trace

3044   track

3045   tractor

3046   to trade

3047   traffic

Bumper to bumper **traffic**

3048   traffic light

3049   trail

The rustlers left a **trail** of hoofprints.

3050   trailer

There is a horse in the **trailer**.

3051   train

3052   to train

She **trained** Spot well.

3053   tramp

3054   to trample

Do not **trample** the flowers!

3055   trampoline

3056   transparent

The glass is **transparent**.

3057   to transport

3058   transporter

3059   trap

3060   trapeze

Aunt Vera takes a lot of luggage when she **travels.**

3061   to **travel**

A **tray** full of drinks

3062   **tray**

3063   **tread**

3064   **treasure**

3065   **tree**

Judith **trembles** with fear.

3066   to **tremble**

3067   **trench**

3068   **trial**

A **triangle** has three sides.

3069   **triangle**

3070   **trick**

The water **trickles** down.

3071   to **trickle**

3072   **tricycle**

3073   **trigger**

3074   to **trim**

3075   a short **trip**

3076   to **trip**

3077   **trolley bus**

Colts like to **trot** and to gallop.

3078   to **trot**

3079   **trough**

3080   **trousers**

3081 trout	3082 trowel	3083 truck	Is it **true** that Ashley swam across the ocean? **True** or false? Is that a **true** story? 3084 true
3085 trumpet	3086 trunk	3087 trunk	3088 trunk
They **trust** each other. 3089 to trust	I am glad you told the **truth**. 3090 truth	**Try** to remember where you put your things. Ashley, do not **try** my patience! You must **try** again. 3091 to try	3092 tub
3093 tube	**Tuesday** is the day after Monday. On **Tuesdays**, Ashley has piano lessons. 3094 Tuesday	3095 to tug	**Tulips** blossom in the spring. 3096 tulip
3097 to tumble	3098 tunnel	3099 turkey	3100 to turn

3101   to **turn off**

3102   to **turn on**

3103   to **turn out**

Chuck **turned out** to be a bad boy.

Things **turned out** well.

3104   to **turn over**

Cheryl **turns over** the steak.

3105   turnip

3106   turntable

3107   turquoise

3108   turret

3109   turtle

3110   tusk

3111   tweezers

3112   twice

Ashley has been to the zoo **twice**.

Curtis has **twice** as many books as me.

3113   twig

There is a leaf on the **twig**.

3114   twins

3115   Stars **twinkle**.

3116   to **twirl**

3117   to **twist**

3118   two

3119   to **type**

Dad **types** all day.

3120   typewriter

She is **ugly** but kind.

3121 ugly

3122 umbrella

My **uncle** is my mother's brother.

My other **uncle** is my father's brother.

3123 uncle

I am not going **under** any circumstances.

Ashley is hiding **under** the covers.

Children **under** 5 cannot go.

3124 under

Harry **understands** the meaning of life.

3125 to understand

3126 underwear

3127 to undress

3128 unhappy

Unicorns appear in fables.

3129 unicorn

Uncle Rick wears a **uniform**.

3130 uniform

Antonia was a good student at **university**.

3131 university

3132 to unload

3133 to unlock

3134 to unwrap

3135 upright

3136 upside-down

Mum **uses** pepper for cooking.

3137 to use

She has **used up** all the pepper.

3138 to use up

A very **useful** pocket knife

3139 useful

A **holiday** in the sun

3140   vacation

3141   vapor/vapour*

Jim **varnishes** the wood to protect it.

3142   to varnish

3143   vase

3144   veal

There are hundreds of tasty **vegetables.**

3145   vegetable

A motor **vehicle**

3146   vehicle

Pat wears a **veil** over her face.

3147   veil

Veins carry blood back to your heart.

3148   vein

Venom is the poison found in some snakes.

Some insects also have **venom.**

3149   venom

A straight line up and down is **vertical.**

3150   vertical

Ashley thinks her brother Carl is **very** clever.

Very soon the soup will be ready.

Spot is a **very** nice dog.

3151   very

3152   vest

We take our sick animals to the **vet.**

3153   veterinarian

The **victim** of a crime

3154   victim

Some people call it a VCR.

3155   video recorder

This is not how you use a **video tape**.

3156   video tape

When Emily and Ashley went camping, they had a nice **view** from the top of the mountain.

We each have our own point of **view.**

3157   view

3158   village

3159 villain

Grapes grow on a **vine**.

3160 vine

Ashley likes **vinegar** on her chips.

3161 vinegar

3162 violet

3163 violin

You need a **visa** to travel abroad.

3164 visa

There are many clouds tonight and the stars are barely **visible**.

The invisible man is not **visible** at all.

3165 visible

Roy **visits** his sick aunt.

3166 to visit

3167 visor

Someone who has a good **vocabulary** knows many words.

A good **vocabulary** is very important.

This dictionary helps increase your **vocabulary**.

3168 vocabulary

You can use your **voice** to sing.

3169 voice

3170 volcano

3171 volleyball

3172 volunteer

3173 to vomit

People **vote** to choose the Prime Minister.

3174 to vote

3175 voter

A, E, I, O, and U are the only **vowels** in the alphabet.

3176 vowel

A long sea **voyage**

3177 voyage

3178 vulture

Bert **wades** right in.

3179   to wade

3180   waffle

3181   wagon

3182   to wail

3183   waist

Carole **waits** for the bus.

3184   to wait

Mum **wakes** him up.

3185   to wake

3186   to walk

3187   wall

3188   wallet

3189   walnut

3190   walrus

A magic **wand**

3191   wand

Ernest **wanders** freely round the countryside.

3192   to wander

Who **wants** more cereal?

Dad **wants** Ashley to help with the washing up.

She **wants** to help but there is no water.

3193   to want

Ashley hates **war**.

3194   war

3195   wardrobe

All sorts of things are stored in this **warehouse**.

3196   warehouse

A jumper and gloves should keep anyone **warm**.

3197   warm

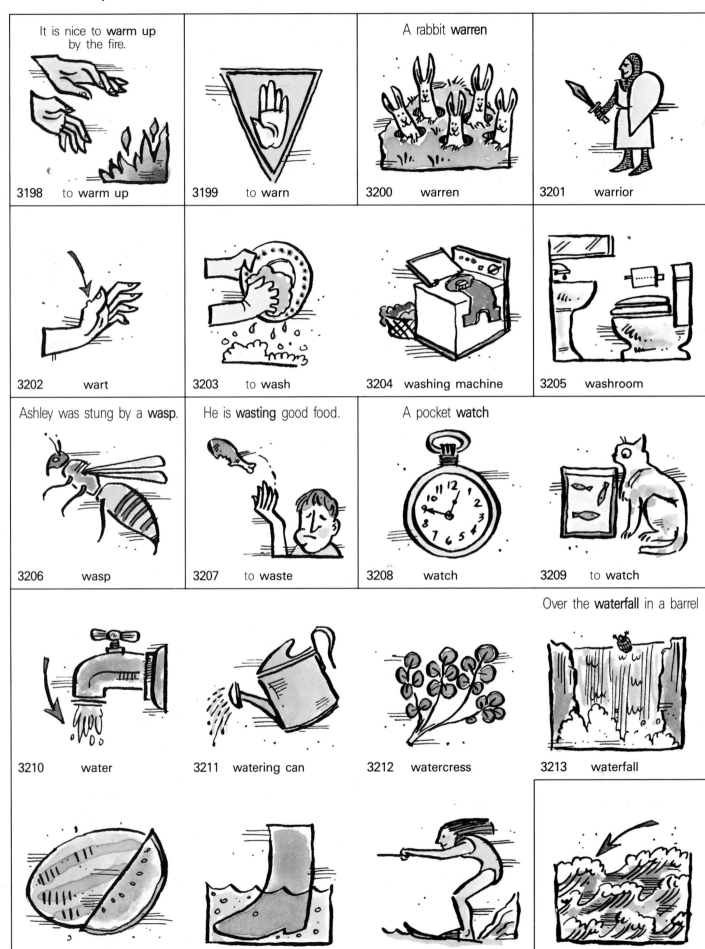

It is nice to **warm up** by the fire.

3198 to **warm up**

3199 to **warn**

A rabbit **warren**

3200 **warren**

3201 **warrior**

3202 **wart**

3203 to **wash**

3204 **washing machine**

3205 **washroom**

Ashley was stung by a **wasp**.

3206 **wasp**

He is **wasting** good food.

3207 to **waste**

A pocket **watch**

3208 **watch**

3209 to **watch**

3210 **water**

3211 **watering can**

3212 **watercress**

Over the **waterfall** in a barrel

3213 **waterfall**

3214 **watermelon**

3215 **waterproof**

3216 **waterskiing**

3217 **wave**

Kay **waves** to her friends.

3218 to **wave**

She has **wavy** hair.

3219 **wavy**

Candles are made from **wax**.

3220 **wax**

Mel is not as strong as his brothers.

3221 **weak**

Weapons are dangerous.

3222 **weapon**

Fred **wears** a hat and gloves with his coat.

3223 to **wear**

3224 **weasel**

What is the **weather** like?

3225 **weather**

3226 to **weave**

3227 **web foot**

3228 **wedding**

3229 **wedge**

Wednesday is the middle of the week.

On **Wednesdays**, Ashley takes out the rubbish.

3230 **Wednesday**

There is a **weed** in the garden.

3231 **weed**

Each **week** has seven days.

3232 **week**

Aunt Vera will visit us this **weekend**.

Saturday and Sunday make a **weekend**.

The weather forecast says it will rain this **weekend**.

3233 **weekend**

He **weeps** because he is sad.

3234 to **weep**

3235 to **weigh**

This picture is **weird**!

3236 **weird**

Kimberly **welcomes** her friend into the house.

3237 to **welcome**

3238   well

3239   I feel well.

West is to the left when North is up.

3240   west

3241   wet

3243   whale

3244   wharf

What has happened to Tigger's fur?

Ashley, what did you do to your cat?

What is it with you?.

3245   what

3242   to wet

3246   wheat

3247   wheel

3248   wheelbarrow

3249   wheelchair

When is Aunt Vera coming, Dad?

When the weekend starts.

When is that?

3250   when

We are lost and Mum has no idea where we are.

Where is the map?

I know where it is but I cannot find it.

3251   where

3252   which one

3253   to whine

3254   whip

3255   whippoorwill

3256   whisk

Cats have whiskers.

3257   whisker

Ashley **whispers** in her friend's ear.

3258   to **whisper**

3259   **whistle**

3260   to **whistle**

3261   **white**

3262   **Who** is going?

I want to know **why** Ashley took my tie.

Why can she not remember?

3263   **why**

The **wick** burns slowly.

3264   **wick**

3265   **wicked**

3266   **wide**

Mrs. Johnson is Mr. Johnson's **wife**.

3267   **wife**

3268   The lion is a **wild** animal.

3269   **willow**

Flowers **wilt** if you forget to water them.

3270   to **wilt**

3271   **wily**

3272   to **win**

Herb **winced** with pain.

3273   to **wince**

3274   **wind**

Wind it up!

3275   to **wind**

3276   **windbreaker**

3277   **windmill**

		Wine is for adults.	
3278 window	3279 windshield	3280 wine	3281 wing

The owl is **winking** at you.		Wipe it clean, please.	Birds on the **wire**
2182 to wink	3283 winter	3284 to wipe	3285 wire

Grandfather is a **wise** old man. Do you think that it is **wise** for Ashley to walk in the forest alone?	I **wish** I could be happy for the rest of my life.		
3286 wise	3287 to make a **wish**	3288 witch	3289 wizard

	A man and a **woman**		A **wonderful** firework display.
3290 wolf	3291 woman	3292 to wonder	3293 wonderful

Woodpeckers eat insects.

| 3294 wood | 3295 woodpecker | 3296 woods | 3297 woodwork |

3298 wool	He said a strange **word**. 3299 word	There are many different kinds of **work**. 3300 work	3301 to work
3303 workshop	3304 world	3305 worm	3302 to work out
Mum sometimes **worries** about Ashley. 3306 to worry	3307 wound	3308 to wrap	A flower **wreath** 3309 wreath
3310 wreck	3311 wren	3312 to wrestle	3313 to wring
3314 wrist	3315 wristwatch	3316 to write	I think our bus is going the **wrong** way. It is **wrong** to cheat and to lie. Are they **wrong** about this? 3317 wrong

3318   X-ray

3319   xylophone

A rather small **yacht**

3320   yacht

We have a nice garden.

3321   yard

Monty **yawns** when he is very tired.

3322   to **yawn**

Another **year**

3323   year

3324   to **yell**

3325   yellow

Yes Virginia, there is a Santa Claus.

Is it **yes**, is it no, or is it maybe?

If you say **yes**, you had better be sure.

3326   yes

Yesterday Ashley was sick from eating too much ice cream.

What did you do **yesterday**?

3327   yesterday

3328   to **yield**

An egg **yolk**

3329   yolk

3330   young

Ashley drew this **zebra**.

3331   zebra

3332   zero

3333   zipper

3334   zoo

3335   to **zoom**

This is my last word.

3336   zucchini

a

abacus 1
about 2
above 3
absent 4
accelerator 5, 1111
accent 6
accident 7
accordion 8
accuse (to) 9
ace 10
ache (to) 11
acid 12
acorn 13
acrobat 14
across 15
add (to) 16
address 17
admiral 18
adore (to) 19
adult 20
advance (to) 21
advantage 22
adventure 23
aeroplane 39
afraid (to be) 24
Africa 25
after 26
afternoon 27
afters 2273
again 28
against 29
age 30
agile 31
aground 32
ahead 33
aid 34
aim (to) 35
air 36
air mattress 37
airtight 38
airplane 39
airport 40
aisle 41
alarm clock 42
album 43
alight 44
alive 45
all 46

alley 47
alligator 48
almond 49
almost 50
alone 51
along 52
aloud 53
alphabet 54
already 55
alright (to be) 56
also 57
aluminium 58
aluminum 58
always 59
ambulance 60
among 61
anchor 62
ancient 63
angle 64
angry (to be) 65
animals 66
ankle 67
announce (to) 68
another 69
answer 70
ant 71
Antarctic 72
antelope 73
antlers 74
any 75
anything 76
anywhere 77
apart 78
ape 79
apiary 80
apologise (to) 81
apologize (to) 81
appear (to) 82, 2625
applaud (to) 83
apple 84
apple core 85
approach (to) 86
apricot 87
April 88
apron 89
aquarium 90
arch 91
architect 92
Arctic 93
argue (to) 94
arm 94

armchair 96
armor 97
armour 97
armpit 98
around 99
arrange (to) 100
arrest (to) 100
arrive (to) 102
arrow 103
artichoke 104
artist 105
as 106
ash 107
ashtray 108
Asia 109
ask (to) 110
asleep 111
asparagus 112
aspirin 113
astonish (to) 114
astronaut 115, 633
astronomer 116
at 117
athlete 118
atlas 119
atmosphere 120
atom 121
attach (to) 122
attention 123
attic 124
aubergine 877
audience 125
August 126
aunt 127
Australia 128
author 129
automatic 130
autumn 131, 945
avalanche 132
avocado 133
awake 134
away (to be) 135
awful 136
awkward 137
axe 138
axle 139

b

baby 140
baby carriage 141
back 142
back up (to) 143
bacon 144
bad 145
badge 146
bag 147
bait 148
bake (to) 149
baker 150
bakery 151
balance 152
balcony 153
bald 154
ball 155
ballerina 156
ballet 157
balloon 158, 159
banana 160
band 161, 162
bandage 163
bang (to) 164
banger 1000
banister 165, 2335
bank 166
banknote 247
bar 167, 168
barbed wire 169
barber 170
bare 171
bargain 172
barge 173
bark (to) 174
bark 175
barley 176
barn 177
barracks 178
barrel 179, 180
barrette 181
barrier 182
base 183, 184
baseball 185
basement 186
basil 187
basket 188
basketball 189
bat 190, 191

bath   194
bath (to take a)   192
bathroom   193
bathtub   194
battery   195
bay   196
bay leaves   197
bazaar   198
be (to)   199
be unable (to)   426
beach   200
bead   201
beak   202
beam   203
beans   204
bear   205
beard   206
beast   207
beat (to)   208
beautiful   209
beaver   210
because   211
become (to)   212
bed   213
bed lamp   214
bedroom   215
bee   216
beech   217
beehive   218
beer   219
beet   220
beetroot   220
beetle   221
before   222
beg (to)   223
begin (to)   224
behave (to)   225
behind   226
beige   227
believe (to)   228
bell   229
belly button   230
belong (to)   231
below   232
belt   233
belt buckle   369
bench   234
bend   235
bend (to)   236
bend down (to)   2828
beret   237

beside   238
besides   239
best   240
better   241
between   242
bib   243
bicycle   244
big   245
bike   246
bill   247
billboard   248
billiards   249
bind (to)   250
binoculars   251
bird   252
birth   253
birthday   254
biscuit   255, 621
bite (to)   256
bite   257
bitter   258
black   259
blackberry   260
blackbird   261
blackboard   262
blackcurrant   263
blacksmith   264
blade   265
blame (to)   266
blank   267
blanket   268
blast   269
blast (to)   270
blaze   271
blazer   272
bleach   273
bleed (to)   274
blender   275
blind   276
blink (to)   277
blister   278
blizzard   279
block   280, 281
block (to)   282
blond   283
blonde   283
blood   284
bloom   285
blossom (to)   286
blot   287
blouse   288

blow   289
blow (to)   290
blue   291
blueberry   292
blunt   293
blush (to)   294
boar   295
board   296
boast (to)   297
boat   298
bobby pin   299
body   300
boil (to)   301
boiler   1902
bolt   302
bone   303
bonfire   304
bonnet   1364
book   305
bookshelf   306
boomerang   307
boot   308
border   309
bore (to)   310, 311
born   312
borrow (to)   313
boss   314
both   315
bottle   316
bottle opener   317
bottom   318
boulder   319
bounce (to)   320
bouquet   321
bow   322
bow tie   323
bowl   324
box   325, 451
boxer   326
boy   327
bra   328
bracelet   329
braces   2883
brag (to)   330
brain   331
brake   332
brake (to)   333
branch   334
brave   335
bread   336
break (to)   337

break down (to)   338
break in (to)   339
breakfast   340
breath   341
breathe (to)   342
brick   343
bricklayer   344
bride   345
bridegroom   346
bridge   347
bridle   348
briefcase   349
bright   350
bring (to)   351
bring back (to)   352
brittle   353
broccoli   354
brooch   355
brook   356
broom   357
brother   358
brow   359
brown   360
bruise   361
brush (to)   362
brush   363, 364, 365
brussels sprout   366
bubble   367
bucket   368
bud   370
buffalo   371
bug   372
bugle   373
build (to)   374
bull   375
bulldozer   376
bullet   377
bullhorn   378
bullock   2809
bully   379
bump   380
bumpers   381
bunch   382
bundle   383
buoy   384
burglar   385
burn (to)   386
burst (to)   387
bury (to)   388
bus   389
bus stop   390

bush 391
busy (to be) 392
but 393
butcher 394
butter 395
butterfly 396
buttons 397
buy (to) 398

C

cabbage 399
cabin 400
cabinet 401
cable 402
cactus 403
cage 404
cake 405
calculator 406
calendar 407
calf 408
call (to) 409
call off (to) 410
call up (to) 411
calm (to be) 412
camel 413
camera 414
camp (to) 415
campsite 416
can 417
can opener 418
canal 419
canary 420
candle 421
candlestick 422
candy 423
cane 424
cannon 425
cannot 426
canoe 427
cantaloupe 428
canyon 429
cap 430
cape 431, 432
capital 433
captain 434, 2666
capture (to) 435
car 436
caravan 437
cards 438

cardboard 439
care (to) 440
careless (to be) 441
cargo 442
carnation 443
carnival 444
carpenter 445
carpet 446
carriage 447
carrot 448
carry (to) 449
cart 450, 3181
carton 451
carve (to) 452
case 453
cash 454
cashew nuts 455
castle 456
cat 457
cataloge 458
catalogue 2687
catapult 458
catch (to) 459
catch up (to) 460
caterpillar 461
cattle 462
cauldron 463
cauliflower 464
cavalry 465
cave 466
ceiling 467
celebrate (to) 468
celery 469
cell 470
cellar 186, 471
cement 472
center 473
centre 473
centimeter 474
centimetre 474
centipede 475
century 476
cereal 477
certain 478
certificate 479
chain 480
chainsaw 481
chair 482
chalet 1680
chalk 483
champion 484

change 485
change (to) 486
channel 487
chapter 488
character 489
charcoal 490
chard 491
charge (to) 492
chariot 493
chart 494
chase (to) 495
chat (to) 496
cheap 497
cheat (to) 498
check (to) 499
check 502
cheek 500
cheese 501
chemist 2096
chemist's 2097
cheque 502
cherries 503
chest 504
chest of drawers 823
chestnut 505
chew (to) 506
chewing gum 1232
chick peas 507
chicken 508
chicken-pox 509
chief 510
child 511
chill 512
chimney 513
chimpanzee 514
chin 515
china 516
chip 517
chisel 518
chives 519
chocolate 520
choir 521
choke (to) 522
choke on (to) 523
choose (to) 524
chop (to) 525
chopsticks 526
chrome 527
chrysanthemum 528
chunk 529
cigar 530

cigarette 531
circle 532
circus 533
city 534
clam 535
clamp 536
clap (to) 537
classroom 538
claw 539
clay 540
clean (to be) 541
clear (to) 542
clever 2698
cliff 543
climb (to) 544
clinic 545
clip (to) 546
clock 547
close (to) 548
closet 549
cloth 550
clothes 551, 1588
clothes line 552
cloud 553
clover 554
clown 555
club 556
clue 557
clutch 558
clutch (to) 559
coach 560, 561
coach (to) 562
coal 563
coarse 564
coast 565
coat 566
cobweb 567
cocoa 568
coconut 569
cod 570
coffee 571
coffin 572
coil 573
coin 574
cold (to be) 575
collar 576
collect (to) 577
college 578
collide (to) 579
collision 580
colors 581

colors 581
colours 581
colt 582
column 583
comb 584
comb (to) 585
combine (to) 586
come (to) 587
come off (to) 588
come to (to) 589
comfortable 590
comma 591
command (to) 592
community 593
companions 594
company 595
compare (to) 596
compass 597
compose (to) 598
composer 599
composition 600
computer 601
concentrate (to) 602
concert 603
concrete 604
conductor 605, 606
cone 607, 608, 609
confident 610
confuse (to be) 611
congratulate (to) 612
connect (to) 613
consonant 614
constable 615
constellation 616
continent 617
conversation 618
cook 619
cook (to) 620
cooker 2836
cookie 621
cool 622
copper 623
copy (to) 624
coral 625
cord 626
cork 627
corkscrew 628
corn 629
corner 630
corpse 631
corridor 632, 1244

cosmonaut 633
costume 634
cot 669
cottage 635
cotton 636
couch 637, 2719
cough (to) 638
count (to) 639
counter 640, 641
country 642, 643
couple 644
courage 645
courgette 3336
court 646
cousin 647
cover (to) 648
cover 649
cow 650
coward 651
cowboy 652
crab 653
crack 654
cracker 655
cradle 656
crane 657, 658
crash (to) 659
crate 660
crawl (to) 661
crayfish 662
crayons 663
cream 664
crease 665
creature 666
creek 667
crew 668
crib 669
cricket 670
criminal 671
crockery 516
crocodile 672
crocus 673
crook 674
crooked 675, 676
crop 677
cross 678
cross (to) 679
cross out (to) 680
crossroads 1453
crow 681
crowd 682
crown 683

crown (to) 684
crumb 685
crush (to) 686
crust 687
crutch 688
cry (to) 589
crystal 690
cub 691
cube 692
cuckoo 693
cucumber 694
cuff 695
cup 696
cupboard 549, 697
curb 698
cured (to be) 699
curl (to) 700
curly 701
curious 702
currant 703
current 704
curtains 705
curve 706
cushion 707
customer 708
cut (to) 709
cut in (to) 710
cut out (to) 711
cute 712
cutlery 713
cycle 714
cylinder 715
cymbals 716
cypress 717

d

daffodil 718
dagger 719
daily 720
dairy 721
daisy 722
dam 723
damaged 724
damp 725
dance (to) 726
dancer 727
dandelion 728
danger 729

dark 730
dart 731
dashboard 732
date 733
daughter 734
day 735
dead 736
deaf 737
dear 738
December 739
decide (to) 740
deck 741
decorate (to) 742
decoration 743
deep 744
deer 745
deliver (to) 746
dent (to) 747
dentist 748
department store 749
desert 750
desk 751
dessert 752
destroy (to) 753
destroyer 754
detective 755
dew 756
diagonal 757
diagram 758
diamond 759
diaper 760
diary 761
dictionary 762
die (to) 763
difference 764
different 765
dig (to) 766
digest (to) 767
dim 768
dimple 769
dinghy 770
dining room 771
dinner 772, 2875
dinosaur 773
direction 774
dirt 775
dirty 776
disagree (to) 777
disappear (to) 778
disaster 779
discover (to) 780

discuss (to) 781
disease 782
disguise 783
disgusting 1215
dish 784
dishonest 785
dishwater 786
dislike (to) 787
dissolve (to) 788
distance 789
distant 790
district 791
ditch 792
dive (to) 793
divide (to) 794
dizzy (to be) 795
do (to) 796
dock 797
doctor 798
dog 799
doll 800
dolphin 801
dome 802
donkey 803
door 804
doorknob 805
double 806
dough 807
dove 808
down 809
doze (to) 810
dozen 811
drag (to) 812
dragon 813
dragonfly 814
drain 815
draw (to) 816
drawbridge 817
drawer 818
dream 819
dream (to) 820
dress 821
dress (to) 822
dresser 823
dessmaker's
  dummy 1056
dribble (to) 824
drift (to) 825
drill (to) 826
drill 827
drink 828

drink (to) 829
drip (to) 830
drive (to) 831
driver 832
drizzle 833
drool (to) 834
drop 835
drop (to) 836
drop in (to) 837
drop off (to) 838
drop out (to) 839
drowsy (to be) 840
drum 841
dry 842
dry (to) 843
dry cleaner 844
dryer 845
duchess 846
duck 847
duel 848
duke 849
dump 850
dump (to) 851
dumptruck 852
dungeon 853
dusk 854
dust 855
dust bin 1104
dwarf 856

e

each 857
eagle 858
ear 859
early 860
earn (to) 861
Earth 862
earth 863
earthquake 864
easel 865
east 866
easy 867
eat (to) 868
eat breakfast 869
eat lunch 870
eat dinner 871
echo 872
eclipse 873

edge 874
eel 875
egg 876
eggplant 877
eiderdown 2319
eight 878
eighth 879
elastic 880
elbow 881
election 882
electrician 883
electricity 884
elephant 885
elevator 886
elk 887
elm 888
embarrass (to) 889
embrace (to) 890
embroidery 891
emergency 892
empty 893
end 894
enemy 895
engine 896
engine driver 897
engineer 897
enjoy (to) 898
enormous 899
enough (to be) 900
enter (to) 901
entrance 902
envelope 903
equal 904
equator 905
errand 906
escalator 907
escape (to) 908
Europe 909
evaporation 910
even 911, 912
evergreen 913
every 914
exam 915
examine (to) 916
example 917
exclamation mark 918
excuse (to) 919
exercise (to) 920
exist (to) 921
exit (to) 922
expand (to) 923

expect (to) 924
expensive 925
experiment 926
expert 927
explain (to) 928
explore (to) 929
explosion 930
extinguisher 931
eye 932
eyebrow 933
eyeglasses 934
eyelash 935

f

fable 936
face 937
factory 938
fail (to) 939, 940
fair 941
fairy 942
faith 943
fake 944
fall 945
fall (to) 946
fall down (to) 947
fall off (to) 948
false 949
family 950
famous 951
fan 952
fancy 953
fang 954
far (to be) 955
farewell 956
farm 957
farmer 958
fast 959
fasten (to) 960
fat 961
fatal 962
father 963
faucet 964
fault 965
favor 966
favorite 967
favour 966
favourite 967
fear (to) 968

feast 969
feather 970
February 971
feed (to) 972
feel (to) 973
female 974
fence 975
fender 976
fern 977
ferry 978
festival 979
fever 980
few 981
field 982
fifth 983
fight (to) 984
file 985
fill (to) 986
fill up (to) 987
film 988, 1851
filthy 989
fin 990
fine 991, 992
finger 993
fingernail 1869
fingerprint 994
finish (to) 995
fir 996
fire 997
fire engine 998
fire escape 999
firecracker 1000
firefighter 1001
fireplace 1002
firm 1003
first 1004
first year 1177
fish 1005
fish (to) 1006
fishhook 1007
fist 1008
five 1009
fix (to) 1010
flag 1011
flake 1012
flame 1013
flap (to) 1014
flare 1015
flash 1016
flashlight 1017
flask 1018

flat 1019
flatten (to) 1020
flavor 1021
flavour 1021
flea 1022
flee (to) 1023
fleece 1024
flesh 1025
float (to) 1026
flock 1027
flood 1028
floor 1029
flour 1030
flow (to) 1031
flower 1032
flu 1033
fluff 1034
fluid 1035
fly 1036, 1037
fly (to) 1038
foam 1039
fog 1040
fold (to) 1041
follow (to) 1042
food 1043
foot 1044
football 1045
footprint 1046
footsteps 1047
for 1048
force (to) 1049
forehead 1050
forest 1051
forget (to) 1052
forgive (to) 1053
fork 1054
forklift 1055
form 1056, 1177
fort 1057
forward 1058
fossil 1059
foul 1060
foundation 1061
fountain 1062
fox 1063
fraction 1064
fragile 1065
frame 1066
freckle 1067
free 1068
freeze (to) 1069

French horn 1375
fresh 1070
Friday 1071
fridge 1072
friend 1073
frighten (to) 1074
frog 1075
from 1076
front 1077
frost 1078
frown (to) 1079
fruit 1080
fry (to) 1081
frying pan 1082
fuel 1083
full 1084
full stop 2087
fun 1085
fund 1086
funeral 1087
funnel 1088
funny 1089
fur 1090
furnace 1092
furniture 1093
furry 1091
fuse 1094

g

gale 1095
gallery 1096
gallop (to) 1097
game 1098
gander 1099
gang 1100
gaol 1476
gap 1101
garage 1102
garbage 1103
garbage can 1104
garden 1105, 3321
gargle (to) 1106
garlic 1107
garter 1108
gas 1109, 1110
gas pedal 1111
gas pump 1112
gas station 1113

gate 1114
gather (to) 1115
gears 1116
gem 1117
general 1118
generous 1119
gentle 1120
gentleman 1121
genuine 1122
geography 1123
geranium 1124
gerbil 1125
germ 1126
get (to) 1127
get back (to) 1130
get in (to) 1132
get off (to) 1131
get on (to) 1129
get rid of (to) 1128
get up (to) 1133
ghost 1134
giant 1135
gift 1136
gigantic 1137
giggle (to) 1138
gill 1139
ginger 1140
gingerbread 1141
gipsy 1142
giraffe 1143
girl 1144
give (to) 1145
give back (to) 1146
give up (to) 1147
give away (to) 3328
glacier 1148
glad (to be) 1149
glass 1150, 1151
glasses 1152
glide (to) 1153
glider 1154
gloves 1155
glue 1156
go (to) 1157
go down (to) 1158
go in (to) 1159
go up (to) 1160
goal 1161
goat 1162
goggles 1163
gold 1164

goldfish 1165
golf 1166
good 1167
goodbye 1168
goose 1169
gooseberry 1170
gorgeous 1171
gorilla 1172
govern (to) 1173
government 1174
grab (to) 1175
gracious (to be) 1176
grade 1177
grain 1178
gram 1179
grandchild 1180
grandfather 1181
grandmother 1182
granite 1183
grant (to) 1184
grape 1185
grapefruit 1186
graph 1187
grass 1188
grasshopper 1189
grater 1190
grave 1191
gravel 1192
gravity 1193
gravy 2506
graze (to) 1194
gray 1202
grease 1195
great 1196
greedy 1197
green 1198
green bean 1199
greenhouse 1200
greet (to) 1201
grey 1202
grill (to) 1203
grimy 1204
grin (to) 1205
grind (to) 1206
grip (to) 1207
groan (to) 1208
grocer 1209
groceries 1210
groom 1211, 1212
groom (to) 1213
groove 1214

gross 1215
ground 1216
groundhog 1217
group 1218
grow (to) 1219
growl (to) 1220
grown-up 1221
guard 606
guard (to) 1222
guess (to) 1223
guest 1224
guide (to) 1225
guilty 1226
guinea pig 1227
guitar 1228
gulf 1229
gull 1230
gum 1231, 1232
gutter 1233

h

habit 1234
haddock 1235
hail 1236
hair 1237
hairbrush 1238
hairdresser 1239
hairdryer 1240
hairgrip 299
hair slide 181
half 1241
hall 1242
Halloween 1243
Hallowe'en 1243
hallway 1244
halt (to) 1245
hammer 1246
hammer (to) 1247
hammock 1248
hamster 1249
hand 1250
handbag 2294
hand out (to) 1251
hand brake 1252
handcuffs 1253
handicap 1254
handkerchief 1264
handle 1255

handrail 1256
handsome 1257
handy 1258
hang (to) 1259
hang on (to) 1260
hang up (to) 1261
hangar 1262
hanger 1263
happen (to) 1265
happy (to be) 1266
harbor 1267
harbour 1267
hard 1268
hare 1269
harm (to) 1270
harmonica 1271
harness 1272
harp 1273
harsh 1274
harvest (to) 1275
hat 1276
hat-stand 2327
hatch (to) 1277
hatchet 1278
haul (to) 1279
haunted 1280
have (to) 1281
hawk 1282
hay 1283
haze 1284
hazel 1285
hazelnut 1286
head 1287
headband 161
headache 1288
headrest 1289
head teacher 2243
heal (to) 1290
healthy 1291
heap 1292
hear (to) 1293
heart 1294
heat (to) 1295
heater 1296
heave (to) 1297
heaven 1298
heavy 1299
hedge 1300
hedgehog 1301
heel 1302
helicopter 1303

hell 1304
hello 1305
helm 1306
helmet 1307
help (to) 1308
helpless 1309
hem 1310
hemisphere 1311
hen 1312
heptagon 1313
herbs 1314
herd 1515
here 1316
hermit 1317
hero 1318
heroine 1319
herring 1320
hesitate (to) 1321
hexagon 1322
hibernate (to) 1323
hiccough (to) 1324
hiccup (to) 1324
hide 1325
hide (to) 1326
hiding-place 1327
high 1328
high rise 1329
high school 1330
highway 1331
hijack (to) 1332
hill 1333
hinge 1334
hind 1335
hip 1336
hippopotamus 1337
history 1338
hit (to) 1339
hive 1340
hoard (to) 1341
hoarding 248
hoarse 1342
hobby 1343
hockey 1344
hockey puck 1345
hockey stick 1346
hoe 1347
hold (to) 1348
hold down (to) 1349
hole 1350
holiday 1351, 3140
hollow 1352

holly 1353
holy 1354
home 1355
homework 1356
honest (to be) 1357
honey 1358
honeycomb 1359
honeydew
  melon 1360
honk (to) 1361
honor 1362
honour 1362
hood 1363, 1364
hoof 1365
hook 1366
hoop 1367
hop (to) 1368
hope (to) 1369
hopeless 1370
hopscotch 1371
hop)scotch 1371
horizon 1372
horizontal 1373
horn 1374
French horn 1375
horn 1376
hornet 1377
horse 1378
horseradish 1379
horseshoe 1380
hose 1381
hospital 1382
hot 1383, 1384
hot pepper 1385
hotel 1386
hour 1387
hourglass 1388
house 1389
hovercraft 1390
how 1391
howl (to) 1392
hub cap 1393
huckleberry 1394
huddle (to) 1395
huge 1396
hull 1397
hummingbird 1398
hump 1399
hundred 1400
hungry (to be) 1401
hunt (to) 1402

hurl (to) 1403
hurricane 1404
hurry (to) 1405
hurt (to) 1406
husband 1407
hut 1408
hutch 1409
hyacinth 1410
hymn 1411
hyphen 1412

i

ice 1413
ice cream 1414
ice hockey 1344
iceberg 1415
icicle 1416
icing 1417
idea 1418
identical 1419
idiot 1420
idle 1421
if 1422
igloo 1423
ignition key 1424
ill 1425
illuminate (to) 1426
illustration 1427
important 1428
in 1429
incense 1430
inch 1431
index 1432
indigo 1433
indoors 1434
infant 1435
infection 1436
infectious 1436
inform (to) 1438
inhabit (to) 1439
initials 1440
injection 1441
injury 1442
ink 1443
insect 1444
inside 1445
insist (to) 1446
inspect (to) 1447

inspector 1448
instead 1449
instruction 1450
instructor 1451
insulation 1452
intersection 1453
interview 1454
into 1455
introduce (to) 1456
invade (to) 1457
invalid 1458
invent (to) 1459
invisible 1460
invitation 1461
invite (to) 1462
iris 1463
iron (to) 1464
iron 1465, 1466
island 1467
itch 1468
itch (to) 1469
itchy 1470
ivy 1471

j

jab (to) 1472
jacket 1473, 1474
jagged 1475
jail 1476
jam 1477
jam (to) 1478
January 1479
jar 1480
jaw 1481
jeans 1482
jeep 1483
jelly 1484
jet 1485, 1486, 1487
jewel 1488
jigsaw puzzle 1489
job 1490
jockey 1491
jog (to) 1492
join (to) 1493
joint 1494
joke 1495
judge 1496
juggler 1497

juice 1498
July 1499
jump (to) 1500
jump in (to) 1501
jump leads 1505
jump on (to) 1502
jumper 1503, 1504
jumper cables 1505
June 1506
jungle 1507
junk 1508, 1509
just 1510

k

kaleidoscope 1511
kangaroo 1512
keep 1513
kennel 1514
kerb 698
kernel 1515
kettle 1516
key 1517
kick (to) 1518
kid 1519, 1520
kidnap (to) 1521
kidney 1522
kill (to) 1523
kiln 1524
kilogram 1525
kilometer 1526
kilometre 1526
kilt 1527
kind 1528, 1529
king 1530
kingfisher 1531
kiosk 1532
kippers 1533
kiss (to) 1534
kiss 1535
kitchen 1536
kite 1537
kitten 1538
kiwi 1539
knee 1540
kneel (to) 1541
knife 1542
knit (to) 1543
knob 1544

knock (to)   1545, 2343
knot   1546
know (to)   1547
knuckle   1548
koala bear   1549

l

label   1550
laboratory   1551
lace   1552
lace (to)   1553
ladder   1554
ladle   1555
lady   1556
ladybird   1557
ladybug   1557
ladyfingers   1558
lair   1559
lake   1560
lamb   1561
lame   1562
lamp   1563
lamp-post   1564
lance   1565
land   1566
land (to)   1567
landing   1568
landlord   1569
lane   1570
language   1571
lantern   1572
lap   1573
larch   1574
lard   1575
large   1576
lark   1577
lash   1578
last   1579
last (to)   1580
latch (to)   1581
late   1582
lather   1583
laugh (to)   1584
launch   1585
launch (to)   1586
launchpad   1587
laundry   1588, 1589
launderette   1589

lavender   1590
law   1591
lawn   1592
lawn mower   1593
lay (to)   1594
layer   1595
lazy (to be)   1596
lead   402, 1603
lead (to)   1597
leader   1598
leaf   1599
leak (to)   1600
lean (to)   1601
learn (to)   1602
leash   1603
leather   1604
leave (to)   922, 1605,
   1606
ledge   1607
leek   1608
left   1609
left-handed   1610
leg   1611
legend   1612
lemon   1613
lemonade   1614
lend (to)   1615, 1674
lens   1616
leopard   1617
leotard   1618
less   1619
lesson   1620
let (to)   1621
letter   1622, 1623
lettuce   1624
level   1625
lever   1626
liar   1627
library   1628
licence   1629
lick (to)   1630
lid   1631
lie (to)   1632
lie down (to)   1633
life   1634
lifeboat   1635
lift   886
lift (to)   1636
light   1637
light (to)   1638
lightbulb   1639

lighten (to)   1640
lighthouse   1641
lightning   1642
lightning rod   1643
like (to)   1644
likely   1645
lilac   1646
lily   1647
limb (to)   1648
lime   1649
limit   1650
limp (to)   1651
line   1652
linen   1653
liner   1654
lining   1655
link (to)   1656
lint   1657
lion   1658
lips   1659
lipstick   1660
liquid   1661
list   1662
listen (to)   1663
liter   1664
litre   1664
litter (to)   1665
little   1666
live (to)   1667
lively   1668
living room   1669
lizard   1670
load (to)   1671, 1672
loaf   1673
loan (to)   1674
lobster   1675
lock (to)   1676
lock   1677
locomotive   1678
locust   1679
lodge   1680
loft   1681
log   1682
lollipop   1683
lonely   1684
long   1685
look (to)   1686
loom   1687
loop   1688
loose   1689
lorry   852, 3058, 3083

lose (to)   1690
lotion   1691
loud   1692
loudspeaker   1693
lounge   1669
lounge (to)   1694
love   1695
love (to)   1696
lovely   1697
low   1698
lower (to)   1699
lucky   1700
luggage   1701
lukewarm   1702
lullaby   1703
lumber   1704
lump   529, 1705
lunch   1706
lunchbox   1707
lung   1708

m

magazine   1709
maggot   1710
magic   1711T
magician   1712
magnet   1713
magnificient   1714
magnifying glass   1715
magpie   1716
mail (to)   1717
mail carrier   1718
maize   629
make (to)   1719
makeup   1720
male   1721
mallet   1722
man   1723
mandarin   1724
mandolin   1725
mane   1726
mango   1727
manners   1728
many   1729
map   1730
marble   1731
marbles   1732
march (to)   1733

March 1734
mare 1735
marigold 1736
mark (to) 1737
mark 1738
market 1739
marry (to) 1740
marsh 1741
mash (to) 1742
mask 1743
mass 1744
mast 1745
master (to) 1746
match 1747, 1748
mathematics 1749
matter 1750
mattress 1751
May 1752
maybe 1753
mayor 1754
maze 1755
meadow 1756
meadowlark 1757
meal 1758
mean 1759
measles 1760
measure (to) 1761
meat 1762
mechanic 1763
medal 1764
medicine 1765
medium 1766
meet (to) 1767
meeting 1768
megaphone 378
melon 1769
melt (to) 1770
member 1771
menu 1772
mercy 1773
mermaid 1774
merry 1775
mess 1776
message 1777
messenger 1778
metal 1779
meteorite 1780
meter 1781, 1782
metre 1782
method 1783
metronome 1784

microphone 1785
microscope 1786
microwave oven 1787
midday 1788
middle 1789
midget 1790
midnight 1791
mile 1792
milk 1793
mill 1794
milometer 1936
mind 1795
mine 1796
miner 1797
mineral 1798
minnow 1799
mint 1800
minus 1801
minute 1802
miracle 1803
mirage 1804
mirror 1805
miser 1806
miss (to) 1807
missile 1808
mist 1809
mistletoe 1810
mittens 1811
mix (to) 1812
mixer 1813
moat 1814
mock (to) 1815
mockingbird 1816
model 1817
modern 1818
moist 1819
mold 1842
mole 1820, 1821
moment 1822
Monday 1823
money 1824
monkey 1825
monkfish 1826
monster 1827
month 1828
monument 1829
mood 1830, 1831
moon 1832
moose 1833
morning 1834
mortar 1835

mosaic 1836
mosquito 1837
moss 1838
mother 1839
motor 1840
motorcycle 1841
motorway 1331
mould 1842
mound 1843
mount (to) 1844
mountain 1845
mouse 1846
moustache 1847
mouth 1848
move (to) 1849
movement 1850
movie 1851
mow (to) 1852
much 1853
mud 1854
mule 1855
multiply (to) 1856
mumps 1857
murder (to) 1858
muscle 1859
museum 1860
mushroom 1861
music 1862
musician 1863
mussel 1864
must 1865
mustache 1847
mustard 1866
muzzle 1867

n

nail 1868
fingernail 1869
nail clipper 1870
nail (to) 1871
naked 1872
name 1873
napkin 1874
nappy 760
narrow 1875
nation 1876
natural 1877
nature 1878

naughty (to be)
    1879
navigate (to) 1880
near 1881
neat 1882
necessary 1883
neck 1884
necklace 1885
nectar 1886
nectarine 1887
need 1888
need (to) 1889
needle 1890
neglect (to) 1891
neigh (to) 1892
neighbor 1893
neighbour 1893
neither 1894
neon sign 1895
nephew 1896
nerve 1897
nervous 1898
nest 1899
nettle 1900
never 1901
new 1902
news 1903
newspaper 1904
next 1905
nibble (to) 1906
nice 1907
nickel 1908
nickname 1909
niece 1910
night 1911
nightingale 1912
nightmare 1913
nine 1914
ninth 1915
no 1916
noble 1917
nobleman 1918
nobody 1919
noise 1920
noon 1921
north 1922
nose 1923
number plate 1629
nut 1924
nutcracker 1925
nylon 1926

o

oak 1927
oar 1928
oasis 1929
oblong 1930
observe (to) 1931
ocean 1932
octagon 1933
October 1934
octopus 1935
odometer 1936
odor 1937
odour 1937
off 1938
offer (to) 1939
officer 1940
often 1941
oil 1942
ointment 1943
old 1944
olive 1945
omelette 1946
on 1947
once 1948
one 1949
onion 1950
only 1951
open 1952
open (to) 1953
operation 1954
opossum 1955
opposite 1956
or 1957
orange 1958, 1959
orchard 1960
orchestra 1961
orchid 1962
order (to) 1963
oregano 1964
organ 1965
oriole 1966
orphan 1967
ostrich 1968
otter 1969
ounce 1970
outdoors 1971
outfit 1972
oval 1973
oven 1974

overboard 1975
overcoat 1976
overflow (to) 1977
overshoe 1978
overturn (to) 1979
owe (to) 1980
owl 1981
own (to) 1982
ox 1983
oxygen 1984
oyster 1985

p

pack (to) 1986
package 1987
pad 1988, 1989
paddle 1990
paddle (to) 1991
padlock 1992
page 1993
pail 1994
pain 1995
paint 1996, 1997
paint (to) 1998
paintbrush 1999
painter 2000
painting 2001
pair 2002
pajamas 2302
palace 2003
pale 2004
palette 2005
palm 2006
pan 2007
pancake 2008
panda 2009
panel 2010
panpipe 2011
pansy 2012
pant (to) 2013
panther 2014
pants 2015
papaya 2016
paper 2017
parachute 2018
parade 2019
parallel lines 2020
paralysed 2021

paralyzed 2021
parcel 2022
parent 2023
park 2024
park (to) 2025
parka 2026
parliament 2027
parrot 2028
parsley 2029
parsnip 2030
particle 2031
partner 2032
party 2033
pass (to) 2034
pass out (to) 2035
passage 2036
passenger 2037
passport 2038
past 2039
pasta 2040
paste (to) 2041
pastime 2042
pastry 2043
pasture 2044
patch 2045
path 2046
patient (to be) 2047
patient 2048
pattern 2049
pause (to) 2050
pavement 2051
paw 2052
pay (to) 2053
pay phone 2054
peace 2055
peach 2056
peacock 2057
peak 2058
peal 2059
peanut 2060
pear 2061
pearl 2062
peas 2063
peat 2064
pebble 2065
pecan 2066
peck (to) 2067
pedal 2068
pedal (to) 2069
pedestrian 2070

pedestrian crossing 2071
peel (to) 2072
pelican 2073
pen 2074
pencil 2075
pendulum 2076
penguin 2077
penknife 2078
pennant 2846
pentagon 2079
people 2080
pepper 2081
peppermint 2082
perch 2083, 2084
performance 2085
perfume 2086
period 2087
periwinkle 2088
person 2089
pest 2090
pester (to) 2091
pet 2092
pet (to) 2093
petal 2094
petrol 1110
petrol pump 1112
petunia 2095
pharmacist 2096
pharmacy 2097
pheasant 2098
phone 2099
phone (to) 411
phone box 2054, 2272
photograph 2100
piano 2101
pick (to) 2102
pick up (to) 2103
pickaxe 2104
pickles 2105
pickle (to) 2106
picnic 2107
picture 2108
pie 2109
piece 2110
piece (to) 2111
pier 2112
pig 2113
pigeon 2114
pigsty 2115
pile 1292, 2116

pill 2117
pillar 2118
pillow 2119
pillowcase 2120
pilot 2121
pimple 2122
pinafore 1504
pincers 2123
pinch (to) 2124
pine 2125
pineapple 2126
pink 2127
pipe 2128
pirate 2129
pistachio 2130
pistol 2131
pitch (to) 2132
pitch 2133
pitchfork 2134
pitch tar 2135
pity (to) 2136
place 2137
plaice 2138
plain 2139, 2140
plan (to) 2141
plane 2142
planets 2143
plank 2144
plant 2145
plant (to) 2146
plaster 2147
plaster (to) 2148
plastic 2149
plasticine 2150
plate 2151
plateau 2152
platform 2153
play (to) 2154
playground 2155
playing cards 2156
plead (to) 2157
pleasant 2158
please 2159
pleat 2160
pliers 2161
plough 2162
plow 2162
pluck (to) 2163
plug 2164, 2165
plug hole 815
plum 2166

plumber 2167
plump 2168
plural 2169
plus 2170
plywood 2171
poach (to) 2172
pocket 2173
pod 2174
poem 2175
poinsettia 2176
point 2177
point (to) 2178
pointed 2179
poison 2180
poisonous 2181
poke (to) 2182
polar bear 2183
pole 2184
policeman 2185
policewoman 2186
polish (to) 2187
polite 2188
pollen 2189
pomegranate 2190
pond 2191
pony 2192
pool 2193
pool (to) 2194
poor 2195
pop (to) 2196
poplar 2197
poppy 2198
popular 2199
porch 2200
pore 2201
porridge 2202
port 2203
portable 2204
porter 2205
portrait 2206
post 1717, 2207
post (to) 2208
post office 2209
postcard 2210
poster 2211
postman 1718
pot 2212
potato 2213
pottery 2214
pouch 2215
pounce (to) 2216

pound 2217
pound (to) 2218
pour (to) 2219
pout (to) 2220
powder 2221
practice (to) 2222
practise (to) 2222
prairie 2223
praise (to) 2224
pram 141, 447
prance (to) 2225
pray (to) 2226
prefer (to) 2227
pregnant (to be) 2228
present (to be) 2229
present 2230
present (to) 2231
preserve 2232
press (to) 2233
pretty 2234
prey 2235
price 2236
prick (to) 2237
prickly 2238
primary school 2239
primrose 2240
prince 2241
princess 2242
principal 2243
principle 2244
print (to) 2245
prism 2246
prison 2247
prisoner 2248
private 2249
prize 2250
problem 2251
produce 2252
produce (to) 2253
program 2254
programme 2254
prohibited 2255
project 2256
promise (to) 2257
prong 2258
pronounce (to) 2259
proof 2260
prop (to) 2261
propeller 2262
properly 2263
property 2264

protest (to) 2265
proud 2266
prove (to) 2267
proverb 2268
provide (to) 2269
prune 2270
prune (to) 2271
pub 168
public 2272
pudding 2273
puddle 2274
puff (to) 2275
puffin 2276
pull (to) 2277
pulley 2278
pullover 2279
pulse 2280
pump 2281
pump (to) 2282
pumpkin 2283
punch (to) 2284
punctual (to be) 2285
puncture (to) 2286
punish (to) 2287
punishment 2288
puppet 2289
puppy 2290
pure 2291
purple 2292
purr (to) 2293
purse 2294
pursue (to) 2295
push (to) 2296
put (to) 2297
put away (to) 2298
put off (to) 2299
putty 2300
puzzle 2301
pyjamas 2302
pyramid 2303
python 2304

q

quail 2305
quality 2306
quantity 2307
quarrel (to) 2308
quarry 2309

quarter 2310
quay 2311
queen 2312
question 2313
quick 2314
quicksand 2315
quiet (to be) 2316
quill 2317, 2318
quilt 2319
quince 2320
quiver 2321
quiver (to) 2322
quiz 2323

r

rabbit 2324
raccoon 2325
race (to) 2326
rack 2327
racket 2328
radiator 1296, 2329
radio 2330
radish 2331
radius 2332
raft 2333
raid 2334
rail 2335
railroad track 2336
railway station 2801
railway track 2336
rain (to) 2337
rainbow 2338
raincoat 2339
raise (to) 2340
raisin 2341
rake 2342
rap (to) 2343
rapid 2344
rare 2345
rash 2346
raspberry 2347
rat 2348
rattle 2349
rattlesnake 2350
raven 2351
ravenous 2352
ravine 2353
raw 2354

ray 2355
razor 2356
reach (to) 2357
read (to) 2358
reading light 214
ready 2359
real 2360
realise (to) 2361
realize (to) 2361
really 2362
rear 2363
rearview mirror 2364
reason 2365
reasonable 2366
rebel (to) 2367
recall (to) 2368
receive (to) 2369
recently 2370
recipe 2371
recite (to) 2372
record 2373
record player 2374
recover (to) 2375
rectangle 2376
red 2377
reed 2378
reef 2379
reek (to) 2380
reel 2381, 2765
referee 2382
reflection 2383
refrigerator 2384
refuse (to) 2385
region 2386
register (to) 2387
regret (to) 2388
rehearse (to) 2389
reindeer 2390
reins 2391
relative 2392
relax (to) 2393
release (to) 2394
remember (to) 2395
remote 2396
remove (to) 2397
rent (to) 2398
repair (to) 2399
repeat (to) 2400
replace (to) 2401
reply (to) 2402
reptile 2403

rescue (to) 2404
reservoir 2405
responsible 2406
rest (to) 2407
restaurant 2408
return (to) 2409
reverse 2410
rhinoceros 2411
rhubarb 2412
rhyme 2413
rib 2414
ribbon 2415
rice 2416
rich 2417
riddle 2418
ride (to) 2419
ridge 2420
right 2421, 2422
right-handed 2423
rind 2424
ring 2425
ring (to) 2426
rink 2427
rinse (to) 2428
riot 2429
rip (to) 2430
ripe 2431
ripple 2432
rise (to) 2433
risk 2434
rival 2435
river 2436
road 2051, 2437
roar (to) 2438
roast 2439
robber 2440
robin 2441
rock 2442
rock (to) 2443
rocket 2444
rocking chair 2445
rod 2446
roll 2447
roll (to) 2448
roller skate 2449
rolling pin 2450
roof 2451
room 2452
roost (to) 2453
root 2454
rope 2455

rose 2456
rosemary 2457
rosy 2458
rotten 2459, 2763
rough 2460
round 2461
row 2462
row (to) 2463
royal 2464
rubber 2465
rubbish 2466
ruby 2467
rudder 2468
rude (to be) 2469
rugged 2470
ruin 2471
rule 2472
ruler 2473
rumble 2474
run (to) 2475
run away (to) 2476
run over (to) 2477
run out (to) 2478
rush (to) 2479
rust 2480
rut 2481
rye 2482

s

sack 2483
sacred 2484
sad 2485
saddle 2486
safe 2487
sail 2488
sailboard 2489
sailboat 2490
sailing boat 2490
sailor 2491
salad 2492
sale 2493
salmon 2494
salt 2495
salute (to) 2496
same 2497
sand 2498
sandal 2499
sandwich 2500

sap 2501
sardine 2502
satellite 2503
satin 2504
Saturday 2505
sauce 2506
sausage 2507
save (to) 2508
saw 2509
saw (to) 2510
sawdust 2511
say (to) 2512
scaffolding 2513
scald (to) 2514
scale 2515
scallop 2516
scalp 2517
scar 2518
scare (to) 2519
scarecrow 2520
scarf 2521
scarlet 2522
scene 2523
scenery 2524
scholarship 2525
school 2526
schooner 2527
scissors 2528
scoop (to) 2529
scooter 2530
scorched 2531
score (to) 2532
scout 2533
scrap 2534
scrape (to) 2535
scraper 2536
scratch 237
screen 2538
screw 2539
screwdriver 2540
scrub (to) 2541
sculptor 2542
seahorse 2543
sea 2544
seagull 2545
seal 2546
seam 2547
search (to) 2548
searchlight 2549
season 2550
seat 2551

seatbelt 2552
seaweed 2553
second 2554
secondary
  school 1330
secret 2555
see (to) 2556
see-saw 2557
seed 2558
seem (to) 2559
seize (to) 2560
selfish (to be) 2561
sell (to) 2562
semicircle 2563
send (to) 2564
sensitive 2565
sentence 2566
sentry 2567
September 2568
serve (to) 2569
serviette 1874
seven 2570
seventh 2571
several 2572
sew (to) 2573
sewing machine 2574
shabby 2575
shack 2576
shadow 2577
shaggy 2578
shake (to) 2579
shallow 2580
shampoo 2581
share (to) 2582
shark 2583
sharp 2584
sharpener 2585,
  2586, 2587
shatter (to) 2588
shave (to) 2589
shears 2590
sheath 2591
sheep 2592
sheet 2593
shelf 2594
shell 2595
shelter 2596
shepherd 2597
shield 2598
shin 2599
shine (to) 2600

shingle 2601
shingles 2602
shiny 2603
ship 2604
shipwreck 2605
shirt 2606
shiver (to) 2607
shock 2608
shoes 2609
shoelace 2610
shoemaker 2611
shoot (to) 2612
shop 2613, 2832
shopkeeper 2614
shop window 2615
shore 2616
short 2617
shorts 2618
shoulder 2619
shout (to) 2620
shove (to) 2621
shovel 2622
show (to) 2623
show off (to) 2624
show up (to) 2625
shower 2626
shriek (to) 2627
shrimp 2628
shrink (to) 2629
shrub 2630
shuffle (to) 2631
shutters 2632
shy 2633
sick 2634
sick (to be) 2987
side 2635
sideboard 1409
sidewalk 2636
sigh (to) 2637
sign 2638
signal (to) 2639
signature 2640
silent 2641
sill 2642
silly 2643
silver 2644
simple 2645
sing (to) 2646
singular 2647
sink 2648
sink (to) 2649

sip (to) 2650
siren 2651
sister 2652
sit (to) 2653
six 2654
sixth 2655
size 2656
skate (to) 2657
skateboard 2658
skeleton 2659
sketch 2660
ski 2661
ski (to) 2662
skid (to) 2663
skin 2664
skip (to) 2665
skipper 2666
skirt 2667
skull 2668
sky 2669
skylark 2670
skyscraper 2671
slam (to) 2672
slanting 2673
slap (to) 2674
slash (to) 2675
slate 2676
sled 2677
sleep (to) 2678
sleeping bag 2679
sleepy 2680
sleet 2681
sleeve 2682
sleigh 2677
slice 2110
slide 2683
slim 2684
slimy 2685
sling 2686
slingshot 2687
slip (to) 2688
slipper 2689
slippery 2690
slob 2691
slope 2692
slot 2693
slouch (to) 2694
slow down (to) 2695
slush 2696
small 2697
smart 2698

smash (to)   2699
smear (to)   2700
smell (to)   2701
smelly   2702
smoke (to)   2703
smooth   2704
snack (to have)   2705
snail   2706
snake   2707
snap (to)   2708
sneakers   2709
sneeze (to)   2710
snooker   249
snorkel   2711
snow   2712
snowflake   2713
snowshoes   2714
soap   2715
soccer   2716
sock   2717
socket   2718
sofa   637, 2719
soft   2720
soldier   2721
sole   2722
solve (to)   2723
somersault (to)   2724
son   2725
song   2726
soon   2727
sorcerer   2728
sore (to be)   2729
sorrel   2730
sorry   2731
sort (to)   2732
soup   2733
sour   2734
south   2735
sow   2736
sow (to)   2737
spaceship   2738
spade   2739
spank (to)   2740
spare tire   2741
spare tyre   2741
spark   2742
sparkle (to)   2743
sparrow   2744
speak (to)   2745
spear   2746
spectacles   934

speed up (to)   2747
spell (to)   2748
spend (to)   2749
sphere   2750
spicy   2751
spider   2752
spike   2753
spill (to)   2754
spin (to)   2755
spinach   2756
spine   2757
spiral   2758
spire   2759
spit (to)   2760
splash (to)   2761
splinter   2762
spoiled   2763
sponge   2764
spool   2765
spoon   2766
spot   2767
spout   2768
sprain (to)   2769
spray (to)   2770
spread (to)   2771
spring   2772, 2773, 2774
sprinkle (to)   2775
sprint (to)   2776
spruce   2777
square   2778
squash   2779
squat (to)   2780
squeeze (to)   2781
squid   2782
squirrel   2783
squirt (to)   2784
stable   2785
stage   2786
stain   2787
staircase   2788
stake   2789
stale   2790
stalk   2791
stallion   2792
stamp   2793
stand (to)   2794
star   2795
stare (to)   2796
starling   2797
start (to)   2798

starve (to)   2799
station   2800, 2801
statue   2802
stay (to)   2803
steak   2804
steal (to)   2805
steam   2806
steel   2807
steep   2808
steer   2809
steer (to)   2810
stem   2811
step   2812
step in (to)   2813
step out (to)   2814
stew   2815
stick   2816
sticky   2817
stiff   2818
sting (to)   2819
sting   2820
stink (to)   2821
stir (to)   2822
stockings   2823
stoke (to)   2824
stomach   2825
stone   2826
stool   2827
stoop   2828
stop   2829
stop (to)   2830
stop)over   2831
store   2832
stork   2833
storm   2834
story   2835
stove   2836
straight   2837
strain (to)   2838, 2839
strange   2840
strangle (to)   2841
strap   2842
straw   2843
strawberry   2844
stream   2845
streamer   2846
street   2847
street lamp   2848
street light   2848
stretch (to)   2849
stretcher   2850

strike   2851
strike (to)   2852
string   2853
stripe   2854
strong   2855
student   2856
study (to)   2857
stuff   2858
stump   2859
submarine   2860
subtract (to)   2861
suck (to)   2862
suddenly   2863
sugar   2864
suit   2865
suitcase   2866
summer   2867
sun   2868
Sunday   2869
sundial   2870
sunflower   2871
sunrise   2872
sunset   2873
supermarket   2874
supper   871, 2875
sure   2876
surface   2877
surgeon   2878
surname   2879
surprise   2880
surrender (to)   2881
surround (to)   2882
suspenders   2883
swallow (to)   2884
swan   2885
swap (to)   2886
swarm   2887
sweat (to)   2888
sweater   2279, 2889
sweatshirt   2889
sweep (to)   2890
sweet   712, 2891
sweets   423
swerve (to)   2892
swim (to)   2893
swing   2894
swing (to)   2895
switch   2896
switch (to)   2897
swoop (to)   2898
sword   2899

sycamore 2900
syrup 2901

 t

table 2902
table lamp 1637
tablecloth 2903
tablet 2711, 2904
tack 2905
tackle (to) 2906
tadpole 2907
tail 2908
tailor 2909
take (to) 2910
take apart (to) 2911
take away 2917
take away (to) 2912
take back (to) 2913
take off (to) 2914,
    2915
take out (to) 2916
take-out 2917
tale 2918
talent 2919
talk (to) 2920
tall 2921
tambourine 2922
tame 2923
tan 2924
tangerine 2925
tangled 2926
tank 2927
tanker 2928
tap 964, 2929
tape 2930
tape (to) 2931
tape recorder 2932
tar 2933
target 2934
tarragon 2935
tart 2936
task 2937
taste (to) 2938
tasty 2939
taxicab 2940
tea 2941
teach (to) 2942
teacher 2943

team 2944
teapot 2945
tear 2946
tear (to) 2947
tear out (to) 2948
telegram 2949
telephone 2950
telephone (to) 2951
telescope 2952
television 2953
tell (to) 2954
temper 2955
temperature 2956
ten 2957
tennis 2958
tennis shoe 2959
tent 2960
tenth 2961
terminal 2962
test (to) 2963
thank (to) 2964
thaw (to) 2965
theater 2966
theatre 2966
there 2967
thermometer 2968
thick 2969
thief 2970
thigh 2971
thimble 2972
thin 2973
thing 2974
think (to) 2975
third 2976
thirsty 2977
thistle 2978
thorn 2979
thread 2980
thread (to) 2981
three 2982
threshold 2983
throat 2984
throne 2985
throw (to) 2986
throw up (to) 2987
thumb 2988
thunder 2989
thunderstorm 2990
Thursday 2991
thyme 2992
ticket 2993

tickle (to) 2994
tidy 2995
tie 2996
tie (to) 2997
tie up (to) 250
tiger 2998
tighten (to) 2999
tights 1926
tiles 3000
tilt (to) 3001
timber 1704
time 3002
tin opener 418
tiny 3003
tip (to) 3004, 3005
tiptoe (to) 3006
tire 3007
tired 3008
toad 3009
toast 3010
toaster 3011
today 3012
toe 3013
together 3014
toilet 3015, 3205
tomato 3016
tomb 3017
tomorrow 3018
tongs 3019
tongue 3020
ton 3021
tonsils 3022
tools 3023
tooth 3024
toothache 3025
toothbrush 3026
toothpaste 3027
top 3028, 3029
topple (to) 3030
torch 1017, 3031
tornado 3032
torrent 3033
tortoise 3034
toss (to) 3035
touch (to) 3036
tough (to be) 3037
tow (to) 3038
towel 3039
tower 3040
tower block 1329
town 3041

toys 3042
trace (to) 3043
track 3044
tractor 3045
trade (to) 3046
traffic 3047
traffic light 3048
trail 3049
trailer 3050
train 3051
train (to) 3052
trainers 2709
tramp 3053
trample (to) 3054
trampoline 3055
transparent 3056
transport (to) 3057
transporter 3058
trap 3059
trapeze 3060
travel (to) 3061
tray 3062
tread 3063
treasure 3064
tree 3065
tremble (to) 3066
trench 3067
trial 3068
triangle 3069
trick (to) 3070
trickle (to) 3071
tricycle 3072
trigger 3073
trim (to) 3074
trip 3075
trip (to) 3076
trolley bus 3077
trot (to) 3078
trough 3079
trousers 2015, 3080
trout 3081
trowel 3082
truck 3083
true 3084
trumpet 3085
trunk 3086, 3087,
    3088
trust (to) 3089
truth 3090
try (to) 3091
tub 3092

tube   3093
Tuesday   3094
tug (to)   3095
tulip   3096
tumble (to)   3097
tunnel   3098
turkey   3099
turn (to)   3100
turn off (to)   3101
turn on (to)   3102
turn out (to)   3103
turn over (to)   3104
turnip   3105
turntable   3106
turquoise   3107
turret   3108
turtle   3109
tusk   3110
tweezers   3111
twice   3112
twig   3113
twin   3114
twinkle (to)   3115
twirl (to)   3116
twist (to)   3117
two   3118
type (to)   3119
typewriter   3120
tyre   3007

U

ugly   3121
umbrella   3122
uncle   3123
under   3124
understand (to)   3125
underwear   3126
undress (to)   3127
unhappy   3128
unicorn   3129
uniform   3130
university   3131
unload (to)   3132
unlock (to)   3133
unwrap (to)   3134
upright   3135
upside-down   3136
use (to)   3137

use up (to)   3138
useful   3139

V

vacation   3140
vapor   3141
vapour   3141
varnish (to)   3142
vase   3143
veal   3144
vegetable   3145
vehicle   3146
veil   3147
vein   3148
venom   3149
vertical   3150
very   3151
vest   3152
vet   3153
victim   3154
video recorder   3155
video tape   3156
view   3157
village   3158
villain   3159
vine   3160
vinegar   3161
violet   3162
violin   3163
visa   3164
visible   3165
visit (to)   3166
visor   3167
vocabulary   3168
voice   3169
volcano   3170
volleyball   3171
volunteer   3172
vomit (to)   3173
vote (to)   3174
voter   3175
vowel   3176
voyage   3177
vulture   3178

W

wade (to)   3179
waffle   3180
wagon   3181
wail (to)   3182
waist   3183
waistcoat   3152
wait (to)   3184
wake (to)   3185
walk (to)   3186
walking stick   424
wall   3187
wallet   3188
walnut   3189
walrus   3190
wand   3191
wander (to)   3192
want (to)   3193
war   3194
wardrobe   3195
warehouse   3196
warm   3197
warm up (to)   3198
warn (to)   3199
warren   3200
warrior   3201
wart   3202
wash (to)   3203
washing
    machine   3204
washroom   3205
wasp   3206
waste (to)   3207
watch   3208
watch (to)   3209
water   3210
watering can   3211
watercress   3212
waterfall   3213
watermelon   3214
waterproof   3215
waterskiing   3216
wave   3217
wave (to)   3218
wavy   3219
wax   3220
weak   3221
weapon   3222
wear (to)   3223

weasel   3224
weather   3225
weave (to)   3226
web foot   3227
wedding   3228
wedge   3229
Wednesday   3230
weed   3231
week   3232
weekend   3233
weep (to)   3234
weigh (to)   3235
weird   3236
welcome (to)   3237
well   3238
well (to feel)   3239
west   3240
wet   3241
wet (to)   3242
whale   3243
wharf   3244
what   3245
wheat   3246
wheel   3247
wheelbarrow   3248
wheelchair   3249
when   3250
where   3251
which   3252
whine (to)   3253
whip   3254
whippoorwill   3255
whisk   3256
whisker   3257
whisper (to)   3258
whistle   3259
whistle (to)   3260
white   3261
who   3262
why   3263
wick   3264
wicked   3265
wide   3266
wife   3267
wild   3268
willow   3269
wilt (to)   3270
wily   3271
win (to)   3272
wince (to)   3273
wind   3274

wind (to)   3275
windbreaker   3276
windmill   3277
window   3278
windscreen   3279
windshield   3279
windsurfer   2489
wine   3280
wing   3281
wink (to)   3282
winter   3283
wipe (to)   3284
wire   3285
wise   3286
wish   3287
witch   3288
wizard   3289
wolf   3290
woman   3291
wonder (to)   3292
wonderful   3293
wood   3294
woodpecker   3295
woods   3296
woodwork   3297
wool   3298
word   3299
work   3300
work (to)   3301
work out (to)   3302
workshop   3303
world   3304
worm   3305
worry (to)   3306
wound   3307
wrap (to)   3308
wreath   3309
wreck   3310
wren   3311
wrestle (to)   3312
wring (to)   3313
wrist   3314
wristwatch   3315
write (to)   3316
wrong   3317

x

x-ray   3318

xylophone   3319

y

yacht   3320
yard   3321
yawn (to)   3322
year   3323
yell (to)   3324
yellow   3325
yes   3326
yesterday   3327
yield (to)   3328
yolk   3329
young   3330

z

zebra   3331
zero   3332
zip   3333
zipper   3333
zoo   3334
zoom (to)   3335
zucchini   3336